DIMENSIONS OF SEA POWER
Strategic Choice in the Modern World

DIMENSIONS OF SEA POWER

Strategic Choice in the Modern World

Edited by Eric Grove and Capt. Peter Hore, RN

THE
UNIVERSITY
OF HULL
PRESS
Cottingham Road
Hull
HU6 7RX

A CIP catalogue record for this book is available from the British
Library.

© **Royal Navy Defence Studies**

Published 1998

Hardback ISBN 0 85958 680 4
Paperback ISBN 0 85958 673 1

Printed by LSL Press Ltd, Bedford

CONTENTS

The Royal Navy's Head of Defence Studies explains how the benefits
of maritime power and its relevance to the United Kingdom's current
strategic needs are helping shape the current review of defence policy.

This chapter explains that the principles of maritime strategy, rooted
in experience of centuries of maritime warfare, still apply in the
application of sea power in the world today. It also emphasises the
joint nature of maritime power and the meaning of the basic terms
used in discussing the subject.

This summarises Professor Gray's thesis that sea power gives its
possessors disproportionate strength to sustain and further their
strategic interests on a global scale. Sea power is not enough on its
own but it plays an indispensable, enabling role in knitting together
maritime coalitions which have been able to defeat more purely
continental opponents throughout the Twentieth Century.

The world's leading expert on the subject provides an up-to-date
account of the latest developments in naval technology and its
impact on maritime operations both at sea and in the littoral
environment. He emphasises the potential of co-operative
engagement capability (CEC) to knit together forces ashore and
afloat in a powerful joint capability.

Commander Steven Haines, a serving officer and also an expert in
law of the sea, describes how law effects maritime operations. He
also assesses how rules of engagement can be used to direct maritime
forces effectively.

distinctive attributes and likely future developments in an area that is likely to be of increasing importance.

The pre-eminent historian of the Royal Navy in the Nineteenth Century explains the ways in which it acted as the core of British strategy between 1815 and 1914; how the Navy secured a global empire and deterred threats to the UK and other British interests in a most cost-effective manner. The chapter demonstrates the essential nature of British maritime strategy in this period, which, as today, emphasised power projection in a littoral environment.

An Australian serving officer, commanding officer of HMAS Sydney, with a deep understanding of the Royal navy past and present, gives a typically discerning view of the contemporary Royal Navy, its strengths and weaknesses. He points out the challenges it faces in ensuring popular understanding of its roles and utility, in sustaining internal understanding of its place in UK society and in convincing the rest of the world of its continued status as a highly-capable and professional force.

Jan Breemer, a lecturer at the United States Naval Postgraduate School, gives a well-balanced overview of the historical and contemporary context of Anglo-American maritime and naval relations, a alliance arguably found at the heart of the wider Anglo-American 'special relationship.' The paper looks at the current strength of the US Navy/Royal navy connection, and the role of this link in protecting and nurturing the roots of the wider transatlantic security linkage.

This concluding chapter demonstrates the likely positive in the Royal Navy's force in the context of current Government defence policy. It discusses the likely developments in the various types of asset, especially the importance of carrier replacement and the need for new, capable anti-air warfare ships. It emphasises the importance of the unique and fundamental contribution the UK's maritime forces make to her continuing role as a leading contributor to the maintenance of international peace and security on a global scale.

Acknowledgements

Many people have assisted with the writing and production of this volume. It may not be possible to recall each of them, and the editors wish to start with a general 'thank you' to everyone involved in this project.

Considerable thanks go to Dr Lee Willett of the Centre for Security Studies, University of Hull, for his role in co-ordinating the project. Glen Innes, of the University of Hull Press, has adhered heroically to the production timescale, and has also cheerfully endured and absorbed delays in writing. Fiona Paton, of the Department of War Studies, King's College, London, has ably co-ordinated the conference (scheduled for February 1998) which marked the launch of the book. The Department of War Studies must be thanked for hosting the conference itself. The Centre for Maritime Policy, University of Wollongong also provided Dr Eric Grove with time and facilities, within the context of his visiting fellowship, to write and edit the volume. The editors wish also to thank the secretariats at both the Directorate of Naval Staff Duties, Ministry of Defence and the Department of Politics, University of Hull. Finally, we would like to thank Admiral of the Fleet Sir Julian Oswald GCB (former First Sea Lord, 1989-1993) for writing the foreword, and him and Sir Patrick Duffy, Ph.D. (Navy Minister under the last Labour government) for kindly agreeing to host the conference marking the launch of Dimensions of Sea Power.

The views expressed in the chapters contained herein are the responsibility of the authors alone. They are not necessarily representative of the views or policies of the Ministry of Defence, Her Majesty's Government, the United States Government or Navy, the Australian Government or Royal Australian Navy or the University of Hull.

EJG & PGH
London, January 1998

About the Authors

Tim Benbow was MacArthur Research Associate on the 'Regional Security in a Global Context' programme, Department of War Studies, King's College, London when he contributed to this book. He holds a BA and an M.Phil from Oxford University. As a postgraduate, he spent a year at the John F. Kennedy School of Government, Harvard University, and was Lecturer in International Politics at Merton College, Oxford. He is currently at St. Antony's College, Oxford, finishing his doctorate on the impact of air power on naval power.

Jan S. Breemer is an Associate Professor of National Security Affairs at the United States Naval Postgraduate School in Monterey, California, where he lectures in maritime security, naval strategic planning and coalition operations. He has published extensively in those areas, including recently: 'European Naval Power after the Cold War: Some Not So Common Interests and Risks', in G. de Nooy (ed.), *The Role of Naval Forces after the Cold War.* (1996); 'The Burden of Trafalgar: Decisive Battle and Naval Strategic Expectations on the Eve of World War I', in Till, G. (ed.), *Sea Power: Theory and Practice.* (1996); 'The End of Naval Strategy: Revolutionary Change and the Future of American Naval Power' in *Strategic Review*, Spring 1994.

Michael Codner is the Assistant Director (Military Sciences) at the Royal United Services. He was formerly a Commander in the Royal Navy. As a Naval Officer he was an anti-submarine warfare specialist. This focus was reflected during his posting to the Ministry of Defence Concepts Division (1987-8), where he was responsible for long term studies in this field. In his career, he has also carried out significant research on strategic theory and strategic and operational concepts. Other postings include a three–year lectureship at the United States Naval War College, the Ministry of Defence Policy Department, the Directorate of Naval Staff Duties and a Defence Fellowship at the Centre for Defence Studies, King's College, London. During his time on the Naval Staff, he co-wrote and edited *BR1806: the Fundamentals of British Maritime Doctrine* (1995).

Norman Friedman is a naval historian and a consultant on defence affairs. He holds a Ph.D in theoretical solid-state physics from Columbia University, New York. Previously, he was a staff member (and, ultimately, Deputy Director for National Security Affairs) of the Hudson Institute and was a consultant to the Secretary of the United States Navy from 1985 to 1994. His 21 books include: *The Naval Institute Guide to World Naval Weapons Systems* (bi-annual); *British Carrier Aviation* (1987); *The US Maritime Strategy* (1989); *The Post-War Naval Revolution* (1986). He has also been widely published in the defence press, including a monthly column in the US Naval Institute's *Proceedings.*

James Goldrick is a Commander in the Royal Australian Navy and is currently the commanding officer of HMAS *Sydney* (FFG-03). He holds a BA and an M.Litt. Since joining the RAN in 1974, he has experienced a broad naval career culminating in his current appointment. Within the context of his RAN career, he has lectured in naval history and contemporary naval affairs at the US Naval Academy, Annapolis, the Britannia Royal Naval College, Dartmouth and the British National Maritime Museum, Greenwich. As a junior officer, he twice won the *Naval Review* Guiness Prize. His recent publications include: *The King's Ships Were at Sea: the War in the North Sea, August 1914-February 1915*; (co-editor) *Reflections on the Royal Australian Navy*; (co-editor) *Mahan Is Not Enough; No Easy Answers: the Development of the Navies of India, Pakistan, Bangladesh and Sri Lanka.* He has also contributed to several other works.

Colin Gray is Professor of International Politics and Director of the Centre for Security Studies, Department of Politics, University of Hull. Among his previous appointments, he was Assistant Director of the International Institute for Security Studies, London, Director of National Security Studies at the Hudson Institute, New York and founding President of the National Institute for Public Policy, Washington DC. He has served as a consultant to many agencies of the British and US governments. He has also lectured at the universities of Lancaster, York (Canada) and British Columbia. His major publications include: *The Soviet-American Arms Race* (1976); *Strategic Studies and Public Policy* (1982); *Nuclear Strategy and National Style* (1986); *The Leverage of Sea Power* (1992); *Explorations in Strategy* (1996); and *Understanding Modern Strategy* (forthcoming with Oxford University Press). He has also been published widely in defence journals.

Eric Grove is Deputy Director of the Centre for Security Studies, Department of Politics, University of Hull. In 1997-8 he was also

Visiting Fellow at the Centre for Maritime Policy, University of Wollongong, Australia. Previous posts include Deputy Head of Strategic Studies at the Britannia Royal Naval College and lectureships at the Royal Naval College, Greenwich and the United States Naval Academy, Annapolis. A renowned naval historian and contemporary maritime strategist, his publications include: *Vanguard to Trident: British Naval Policy Since 1945* (1987); *The Future of Sea Power* (1990). He was co-author and co-editor of *BR1806: the Fundamentals of British Maritime Strategy* (1995). He has also published widely in defence-related journals.

Steven Haines is a Commander in the Royal Navy and is currently a member of the Naval Staff in the Ministry of Defence, London. In this context he is responsible for the development of the UK's military strategic level maritime doctrine. He holds a first-class honours degree in International Relations with International Law, and his Ph.D. thesis examined the legal arrangements for the conduct of naval operations in Britain's maritime domain. His operational experience commenced with Beira Patrol and includes a total of eight years engaged on coastal security and policing operations.

Peter Hore is a Captain in the Royal Navy and is currently Head of Defence Studies for the Navy in the Ministry of Defence. Having graduated from the Britannia Royal Naval College, Peter Hore was one of the youngest officers ever to graduate from the Royal Naval Staff College, Greenwich. His career began as a logistics and personnel expert in the Royal Navy, developing into specialised study of long-term defence concepts, systems and naval strategy. As Head of Defence Studies, he is responsible for developing the debate on defence and maritime security at universities and institutes of learning. He has published widely on professional matters, naval history and strategy. He is currently a doctoral candidate at the Centre for Maritime Historical Studies, University of Exeter.

Andrew Lambert is Senior Lecturer in War Studies in the Department of War Studies, King's College, London. He holds an MA and a Ph.D from the Department of War Studies, and undertook lecturing responsibilities at Bristol Polytechnic, the Royal Naval College Greenwich and the Royal Military Academy, Sandhurst, before rejoining the Department of War Studies in 1991. He is currently completing a biography of the pioneer naval historian, Professor Sir John Knox Laughton. His recent publications include: *The Crimean War: British Grand Strategy against Russia 1853-1856*.

(1990); *The Last Sailing Battlefleet: Maintaining Naval Mastery 1815-1850.* (1991); *Steam, Steel and Shellfire: the Steam Warship 1815-1905.* (1992); (with Dr S Badsey) *The War Correspondents: the Crimean War.* (1994). He has also written numerous papers and journal articles.

Michael Pugh is Reader in International Relations and Director of the International Studies Research Centre, University of Plymouth. He also currently directs the Plymouth Peacebuilding Project. In 1994-5 he was Economic and Social Research Council Senior Research Fellow. His publications include: *Maritime Security and Peacekeeping: a Framework for UN Operations.* (1992); (editor) *The UN Peace and Force.* (1997). He has also published numerous papers and journal articles on international peacekeeping and European contributions to global security. He is the chief editor of the journal *International Peacekeeping.*

Julian Thompson is Visiting Professor in the Department of War Studies, King's College. He is a retired Major General in the Royal Marines, and commanded 3 Commando during the Falklands War. He was honoured with a CB and an OBE. He has written extensively on military history, his publications including: *No Picnic: 3 Commando Brigade in the Falklands,* (1982); *Ready for Anything: the Parachute Regiment at War, 1940-1982; The Lifeblood of War: Logistics in an Armed Conflict; The Imperial War Museum book of Victory in Europe: North-West Europe 1944-45; The Imperial War Museum book of the War at Sea: the Royal Navy in the Second World War; The Imperial War Museum book of War Behind Enemy Lines* (forthcoming).

Lee Willett is Leverhulme Research Fellow at the Centre for Security Studies, Department of Politics, University of Hull. He holds a BA in International Relations and an MA in War Studies. In 1997, he completed a doctorate on the *Tomahawk* Sea-Launched Cruise Missile and US-Soviet arms control. He worked as Research Analyst at Royal Navy Defence Studies, completing three forthcoming papers on the UK *Tomahawk* programme. Since the completion of this contract, he has remained as Honorary Research Fellow of the Maritime Studies Programme, Royal Navy Defence Studies. He has lectured in Maritime Strategy at the Centre for Security Studies, and continues to undertake contract work for the Royal Navy and Ministry of Defence.

GLOSSARY: ACRONYMS AND TERMS

Acronyms

AAW	Anti-Air Warfare
ABM	Anti-Missile Defence
AD	Air Defence
AEW	Airborne Early Warning
AIP	Air Independent Propulsion
ASW	Anti-Submarine Warfare
ASuW	Anti-Surface Warfare
CAS	Close Air Support
CEC	Co-operative Engagement Capability
CNGF	Common New Generation Frigate
CSCE	Conference on Security and Co-operation In Europe
CVA	Aircraft carrier (large)
CVSG	Aircraft carrier (small)
DSP	Defense Support Project
EFA	European Fighter Aircraft
EURMARFOR	European Maritime Force
EEZ	Economic Exclusion Zone
GPS	Global Positioning System
ICBM	Intercontinental Ballistic Missile
IISS	International Institute for Strategic Studies
IMO	International Maritime Organisation
JOTS	Joint Operational Tactical System
JSF	Joint Strike Fighter
LCAC	Landing Craft Air Cushion (hovercraft)
LCVP	Landing Craft Vehicle and Personnel
LTC	Long Term Costings
LPD	Landing Platform Dock
LPH	Landing Platform Helicopter
LSL	Landing Ship Logistics
MCM	Mine Counter Measures
MIRV	Multiple Independently-Targeted Re-entry Vehicle
NATO	North Atlantic Treaty Organisation
NPT	Non-Proliferation Treaty
OECD	Organisation of Economic Co-operation and Development
OOTW	Operations Other Than War

RAM	Radar-Absorbing Material
RFA	Royal Fleet Auxiliary
RMA	Revolution in Military Affairs
ROE	Rules of Engagement
RUSI	Royal United Services Institute
SAS	Special Air Service
SDR	Strategic Defence Review
SLBM	Submarine-Launched Ballistic Missile
SLEP	Service Life Extension Programme
SSBN	Sub-Surface Ballistic Nuclear (submarine)
SSN	Sub-Surface Nuclear (submarine)
STOVL	Short Take-Off Vertical Landing (aircraft)
TLAM	Tomahawk Land Attack Missile (conventional/nuclear)
UAV	Unmanned Aerial Vehicle
UNCLOS	United Nations Conference on the Law of the Sea
UNTSO	United Nations Truce Supervision Organisation
USMC	United States Marine Corps
USN	United States Navy
UUV	Unmanned Underwater Vehicles
WEU	Western European Union
WMD	Weapons of Mass Destruction

Terms

Air Defence – In the context of aircraft, these will be fixed-wing fighters armed with air-to-air missiles and cannon.

Airborne Early Warning – aircraft fitted with radar to detect enemy aircraft at long range.

Anti-Surface Warfare – In the context of AsuW aircraft, these are helicopters fitted with anti-ship missiles or, in the case of fixed wing aircraft or bombs, and/or rockets.

ASW – In the context of ASW aircraft, these are helicopters or fixed-wing aircraft specially equipped for detecting and attacking submarines, as part of the ASW battle.

Close Air Support – Supporting fire for ground troops provided by combat aircraft.

Commando – Can refer to: a unit of about battalion-size (700 approx); a Royal Marine or Army soldier who has passed the Commando course.

Gazelle – Utility helicopter.

Landing Craft Vehicle and Personnel – Small landing craft capable of taking a land-rover and trailer, or about 30 personnel.

Landing Helicopter Dock – Multi-purpose assault ship, with full-length flight deck and dock in the stern which can be flooded to allow craft to enter and leave through a tail-gate lowered for the purpose.

Landing Platform Helicopter – Aircraft carrier designed to operate helicopters. British LPH designed to carry commando group.

Lynx – Utility helicopter capable of carrying ten troops (depending on equipment worn/carried), or more usually eight TOW anti-tank missiles.

Merlin – Medium lift helicopter. Replacing Sea King with a bigger lift.

MEXEFLOTE – Hollow metal pontoons which, when joined together, will make a 120 or 60 foot raft powered by large outboard engines. The rafts can also be joined together to make a causeway. Acronym stands for Mechanical Engineering Experimental Establishment (where the equipment was developed) flote,

Rigid Inflatable – Glass-fibre hull, and inflatable sides.

Rigid Raiders – Small rigid glass-fibre craft powered by diesel engine.

Ro-Ro – Roll-on Roll-off. Ships, like many cross-channel ferries, which can embark vehicles at one end of the vessel and disembark at the other, obviating the need for vehicles to be turned round inside, or have to reverse in.

Sea King – Medium lift helicopter. Can carry about 25 troops (depending on equipment worn/carried).

TOW – Tube-launched Optically tracked Wire-guided anti-tank missile.

Dimensions of Sea Power:
Strategic Choice in the Modern World

The most far reaching event in world security in the last 40 years has been the collapse of the Berlin wall. That event did not just mark the end of a rift across Europe, but in strategic terms had much wider significance for Britain. Since 1793, through the French Revolutionary and Napoleonic wars, through winning and garrisoning an empire, two world wars, and the alliance system of the Cold War, British strategy has been tied to the need to defend territory. Now, for the first time in over 200 years, Britain is in a position to forge a defence strategy freed from this requirement. Britain has the choice, for the first time in many years, to decide what forces are necessary to meet its wider defence and security wishes and responsibilities.

Publication of *Dimensions of Sea Power: Strategic Choice in the Modern World* could not, therefore, come at a better time. With British defence policy under the microscope of the Strategic Defence Review, the Government is looking for choices of how best to provide the necessary means to meet the United Kingdom's national and international responsibilities and interests, in peace support operations, in the deterrence of hostilities, and, should deterrence fail, in war.

The distinguished authors who have contributed to this book make a happily eclectic list. It is particularly heartening to note the contribution from younger members of the academic and defence community, including members of the armed forces, who have taken a fresh look at some of the key issues that face Britain today.

The inescapable conclusion from my reading of this book is that maritime forces, which throughout history have offered real and enduring flexibility, continue to offer great advantage to a country like ours which is still so dependent upon the use of the seas, and which, for natural and historical reasons, just happens to be good at sea. This book puts the case persuasively that Britain, after pursuing a continental strategy for most of this century, now has an opportunity to return to that enduring rhythm which has always been an essential element of the British way of doing things, namely a maritime strategy.

Admiral of the Fleet Sir Julian Oswald GCB

The Strategy of Choice

Peter Hore

Ten years on

Since the end of the Cold War there has been what the Secretary of State for Defence, George Robertson, called in the debate on Defence in the House of Commons on 27 October, a bonfire of the certainties.[1] In the same debate his junior minister, the Minister for the Armed Forces, John Reid, used another metaphor, "...the Cold War presented grave dangers," he said, "but the two great glaciers held in check in their hinterland a multitude of potential problems, frozen in relative stability ..."[2] So, small wars, which might lead to more serious ones, are more likely than they were during the Cold War; in fact there have been more than 90 armed conflicts throughout the world in the last ten years.

Transnationalism and Globalisation

In the interwar years the world order was measured and nations ranked by their possession or access to raw materials, and the count of battalions and battleships. Even large companies too, which tended to be national in character, could be measured in a similar, simple way. Today "... self-sufficiency is not a [condition] to which nations can reasonably aspire in the modern world ...[where] economic inter-dependence is the norm..."[3] The new world order is governed by transnationalism and globalisation, two factors which lead to a much greater mutual interdependence and the need for a changed understanding of international relations and measures of the wealth, or rank, of nations.

As Richard Rosecrance of UCLA has explained, transnationalism occurs when transactions take place between parties from two different nations, at least one of which is not a government.[4] For example, some large companies have economies larger than the smaller member states of the United Nations, and their economies are widely based, with production in one country, research in another, financial control in a third. Some criminal organisations also have a turnover as large as an international company, access to much human capital and to sophisticated technology. Transnationalism can, of course, occur between a nation-state and a criminal organisation and in turn crime may have links in cross-border issues such as religion or ethnicity. In fact criminal and terrorist organisations can combine to display a kind of deadly synergy in a multi-service agency.[5]

Globalisation represents a new industrial revolution where, in the face of technology and ideology, the state retreats and tends to become the servant rather the master of international markets. The world, it is alleged, benefits from faster technological progress, historically unprecedented opportunities for the relief of global poverty, and greater freedom for millions of people around the globe. According to *The Economist*, only pessimists, "...a coalition of populist conservatives, assorted communitarians and the old Left...", resent globalisation.[6]

These two factors, transnationalism and globalisation, make our world interdependent, but in turn depend themselves upon international means of communication, primarily, of course, on electronic communications and the revolution which has been brought about by the PC and the internet. It appears that advances in computing and telecommunications will press on relentlessly, shrinking distance, eroding national boundaries and enlarging the domain of the global economy.

Trade and Investment

There is however no substitute for the physical transfer of goods between trading partners. In 1994 there were over 27,000 merchant ships some 700 million DWT. 9,000 of these ships entered and left the Indian Ocean via the so-called chokepoints to the West, through the straits of the Indonesian archipelago or the Straits of Malacca, and 4,000 ships entered and left the Indian Ocean via the Red Sea. It may appear that these statistics are of little interest to Britain whose trade today is primarily with Europe, but British and American sources estimate that by beneficial ownership, rather than flag,

4

between one fifth and one quarter of all this shipping is British-owned. Despite British withdrawal from Hong Kong, British interests in the Far East are still large, and, for example, in terms of beneficial ownership British merchant ships form the third largest group, after Japan and Greece, of ships using the sea-lanes which pass the much disputed Spratly Islands in the South China Sea.

The sea route through the South China Sea and via the Spratly Islands to Japan, and to other destinations in the Asia Pacific Rim, is also important to Britain and Europe because trade with East Asian countries is so large and is increasing, given impetus by the generally peaceful conditions there since the end of the Cold War. Over one quarter of European external trade is with East Asia; Europe exports as much to East Asia as does the USA, with over one-quarter of all investment in East Asia being European and Britain alone accounting for 15% of this investment.[7]

Both the World Bank and OECD predict that world merchandise trade, i.e. shipping, will grow by at least at 5-6% per annum to 2005 and beyond. In fact the British Chamber of Shipping predicts that sea-borne trade should double between now and 2010 to over 4,000 billion tonne-miles. This indicates a massive expansion in the value of the world's shipping freight industry, currently valued at some £100bn, an industry in which Britain has a significant stake. It should be noted that there is no technological alternative to the ship for this trade.

British seaborne trade in 1994 amounted to some 95% by volume and nearly 80% by value of all imports and exports with non-EU countries, in value some £217 billions worth, which entered and left the UK by ferry, by bulk carrier and in over 6 million containers. These percentages do not change in peace or war. In the Falklands War as in the Gulf War more than 90% of all equipment was transported by sea, including all the main battle tanks.

Britain is the second biggest overseas investor and the second biggest recipient of inward investment, behind the US in both cases.[8] This makes Britain one of the world's largest trading nations, peculiarly dependent upon foreign trade and investment.

People

In addition to British trade and investment, there are some 10 million Britons living abroad, about 1 million of them in South Africa and 4 million in the Asia Pacific region. As tourists, 34 million Britons travel abroad each year, to ever more distant and exotic places. Another 100 million passengers enter and leave Britain each year, in total about one quarter by sea and three quarters by air. These numbers are a measure of the importance to Britain of another form of trade, inward-tourism, and another demonstration of our need for and reliance upon the sea-lanes and airways of the world for our prosperity and well-being.

The Seas

In addition to trade, the seas are significant to us for other reasons. The seas cover about two-thirds of the world's surface yet comparatively little is known about the riches that may lie below the surface. They have been described as inner-space or, in Ronald Reagan's words, as the last great frontier. In Britain's case, for example, the fishing fleet numbered some 9,000 vessels of all sizes and landed some seven and quarter million tonnes of fish in 1995. As for oil, Britain has been a net exporter of oil since the 1980s. It is likely that as resources on land become scarcer, exploration of the seabed will no longer be neglected and may be carried out in a spirit of intensified competition.

Of the 185 member states of the United Nations, 150 are coastal states, and 70% of the world's population lives within 100 miles of the coast as do almost all of the world's largest cities and industrial complexes. Yet the territorial waters of coastal states are limited to 12 miles from the coast, beyond which are the interconnected seas and oceans which cover nearly three quarters of the world's surface. This area is known, in a legal sense, as the high seas. These seas and oceans of the world are contiguous. Even in territorial waters ships, including warships, have rights of innocent passage. There are even non-suspendable rights of innocent passage through territorial or internal waters and archipelagic seas when these are recognised as international straits. So the seas are relatively free of restrictions, and they form, in the words of Captain Alfred Mahan, "...a great highway ... a wide common over which men may pass in all directions ..."[9] with their goods.

However, even in peacetime there are attempts by coastal states to impose their jurisdiction on the seas. Indonesia for instance makes excessive claims to regulate archipelagic sea lanes and to place restrictions on warships, claims which are unacceptable to the maritime powers. Malaysia claims the right to impose traffic control measures in the Malacca Straits. India has challenged military activity in its exclusive economic zone; and Turkey claims the Black Sea Straits as internal waters, which Russia maintains is contrary to the Montreux Convention. Other states such as China flout internationally agreed criteria for the delineation of baselines: in this case this amounts to excessive claims based on the Paracel Islands in the South China Sea. China is also one of several nations, Vietnam, Taiwan, Philippines, and Malaysia included, which have overlapping claims to the Spratly Islands in the South China Sea, which are not only potentially rich in oil but also lie astride one of the major sea routes of the world.

British Interests

So, Britain, in common with Europe and many other of the world's nations, has strong interests in the ability to trade overseas, in stable trading conditions in each region, and in the freedom to use the sealanes and airways of the world for the transport of goods and people, as well as the exploitation of the seas' resources. "Instability," said George Robertson, the Secretary of State for Defence, during the debate on defence in Parliament on 27th October, "is the enemy that can threaten the peace and prosperity we now enjoy ..."[10]

The Geo-Strategic Situation

Undoubtedly Pax Americana is *the* predominant characteristic of any and all strategic considerations. There is no parallel, or not since Britain's pre-eminence in the 19th century, for the American hegemony on land and sea, in air and space. The USA's defence budget is equivalent to the budgets of the next ten significant military powers added together and its weaponry is in many cases a generation ahead. Yet at US$250B a year it is only 3 1/2 % of GDP. The last time that the USA spent so small a portion of its wealth on defence was in 1940, the year before the Japanese attack on Pearl Harbour - an attack which eventually started the USA on the road to its present global dominance. Or as *The Guardian* newspaper's US correspondent puts it:

> "...The USA is the modern Rome: her garrisons stand watch on the Rhine as the legions did 2000 years ago, but its troops and bases also uphold Pax Americana in Japan, Korea and the Persian Gulf. Its language (and happily ours) is the modern Latin, just as the communications satellites, phone links and the Internet are the modern equivalent of Roman roads. Having won both the hot and cold wars alike, the Americans even have that Roman obsession with the export of decent plumbing and central heating..." [11]

It is this Pax Americana which delivers to us, and the community of nations in general, the freedom of the seas. In the Prime Minister's words, "We must never forget the historic and continuing role of the US in defending the political and economic freedoms we take for granted. Leaving all sentiment aside, they are a force for good in the world."[12] It is no coincidence that this freedom is provided to us and manifested largely though an American strategy which is maritime in character. The relevant documents which describe this strategy are *Forward ... from the sea* and *Joint Vision 2010*. The joint warfare seen by these papers is no longer one which focuses narrowly on the defeat of the former Soviet Union through an attack on its bases, but a maritime strategy in the sense in which Sir Julian Corbett would have meant the phrase.

Undoubtedly the next most important factor, after Pax Americana, is that it is widely considered that there is no threat of general war, and by general war is meant war at the highest level of conflict involving the nation and the application of all its resources to achieve some political end. The threat of general war with which we have lived for the last forty years was from the Soviet Union; today it is widely considered that Russia, for the time being at least, is not capable of invading Europe. In addition, new defence and security regimes are designed to build confidence between the countries of Europe and to remove the threat of war for all time.

Another threat to Western security is terrorism, a shorthand for all forms of criminal as well as ideological violence against the state. Counter-measures however are properly the business of the police and not the armed forces of the state.[13] Thus terrorism is not a problem which will be discussed here, even though specially trained units of the regular armed forces might be called upon in situations, including piracy at sea, where their unique skills are needed.

Yet one more threat is the proliferation of advanced weapons systems. There are already, for example, 46 navies operating some 650 submarines, and over the next few years these are expected to be modernised. The consequences, even if only a few of these nations were successful in operating hostile submarines on the sealanes of the world, say on the route to the Gulf, are easy to imagine. However, perhaps the most significant new threat is the possibility of the proliferation of cruise and ballistic missiles. Limiting the spread of these weapons, and of other weapons of mass destruction (WMD), is the business for diplomacy; it is sufficient here to say that some defensive precautions must be taken in the event of a failure of such diplomacy to prevent the spread of these weapons, particular into the hands of "rogue" states.

So far I have discussed physical properties of the geo-strategic situation. What though are the circumstances under which violence might break out? There is ample literature on the causes of instability, whether they stem from a struggle over resources, oil or water for example, population imbalance, environmental ruin, ethnic, or religious rivalries, to name but a few.

Ethical Interests

It is clear that the consequent instability would be of concern to Britain, Europe and the USA because it might disrupt trade or put investments at risk or harm British citizens. There is of course another reason why Britain would be concerned, and that is the ethical dimension which the Government wishes to give to its foreign policy. If there is to be an ethical dimension to British foreign policy, then it will surely require positive action in resisting aggression, protecting innocent civilians, trying to prevent genocide, terrorism and enforced

9

starvation, assisting refugees and tackling the world-wide scourge of the drugs traffic.[14] These are not just the views of high-minded politicians or of the military seeking institutional survival, but international, non-governmental organisations such as OXFAM who also think that, when confronted by genocide or ethnic cleansing, Britain has a moral duty to intervene.[15] In the words of the Foreign Secretary, Robin Cook, "...you cannot have an ethical foreign policy if it is isolationist ... we cannot stand back when [the] principles [of the United Nations Charter] are being violated..."

Quite apart from the Government's commitment to being internationalist, rather than isolationist, we live in a world which is increasingly interdependent where the politics of isolation or disengagement are not possible or desirable. This is a world where failure to be proactive or to invest in preventive deployments can only lead to spiralling costs later. In any case, Britain's membership of the Security Council, of the Group of 7, of the Commonwealth, as well as of the European Union, and many other bilateral and multilateral defence and security agreements means that we cannot simply stand aside. All of these links give us a particular responsibility for upholding international law and it is clear that on occasions upholding this law will require military intervention.

These factors lead to a paradox. After the Napoleonic Wars Britain was concerned with the defence of a large Empire. At the beginning of this century she became increasing concerned about the rise of hegemonic powers on the continent: first was Germany, then Russia. Finally during the Cold War it was necessary to concentrate on the potential land-air battle in the central region of Europe. During these stages of her history Britain switched from a purely maritime strategy to a continental strategy. Meanwhile the Empire gained its independence. British dependencies now number just 13, about the same as they were in the 17th century. With the threat of war on the continent very much reduced and the dependencies so few, Britain, for the first time in over two hundred years, is free of the onerous responsibility of defending territory in Europe or overseas. The paradox is that there is simultaneously both less threat and less peace.

The Peace Dividend Paid?

With the collapse of the Soviet Union public perceptions regarding the use of their armed forces has shifted towards preventive diplomacy, defence diplomacy,[16] international aid and interdependence. Quite rightly public opinion on the appropriate level of defence spending has changed.[17] The shift in attitude was quite quickly called the "peace dividend," and the dividend in Britain since the end of the Cold War has been large. There are 100,000 fewer men and women in uniform, down from 315,000 to 215,000 (or 32% less than in 1990); the number of infantry battalions has been reduced from 55 to 40; the number of tanks from 699 to 304; the number of RAF aircraft in service is down from 630 to 500; the number of conventionally armed submarines has fallen from 28 to 12; and the number of destroyers and frigates from 48 to 35. In fact the UK's expenditure at 2.7% of GDP is at the lowest level since 1934.

The United States of America not the Sole Arbiter

Given a reduced threat to the United Kingdom mainland, smaller armed forces, less money for defence, and the preponderance of Pax Americana, some might think it possible to leave all defence and security issues outside the immediate environs of Europe to the Americans and to local regional powers. There are four reasons why Britain should lift her eyes.[18]

First, while Britain's immediate interest is in the maintenance of NATO as an effective political and military alliance, she needs peace and stability in the border regions such as the Gulf, the Middle East and North Africa. She must also be prepared to meet challenges to the security of the 13 overseas Dependent Territories, to respond to threats beyond these areas and to other direct calls on British forces, and to meet her international responsibilities. As Stares and Regaud have pointed out, quite apart from trade, investment and expatriate citizens, Britain, by not playing an active security role in the wider world, may risk major commercial opportunities which other nations may seize.

Second, as Stares and Regaud have highlighted in their prominent article in a recent edition of the International Institute for Strategic

11

Studies (IISS) Quarterly, that Britain still has wide ranging security responsibilities in other regions. Using the Asia-Pacific Rim as an example, again, these include: the Korean Armistice in which the US, France and UK are involved; the Five Power Defence Agreement between Australia, Malaysia, New Zealand, Singapore and the UK; troops stationed in Brunei and an agreement to consult the government there in time of tension; and the South East Asia Collective Defence Treaty between Australia, France, New Zealand, Pakistan, the Philippines, Thailand, the US and the UK, a treaty which though in abeyance has never been abrogated. Britain also has a number of bilateral agreements, as well as, of course, an implicit duty to defend the 13 remaining dependencies. Even if some of these security arrangements may be regarded as vestigial, Britain as a member of the Security Council of the United Nations will have a direct interest in the security arrangements of the region and an ongoing, active interest in Asia-Pacific affairs is likely to have a calming and deterrent effect, helping to avoiding greater, more costly involvement in possible conflicts later.

Third, there are several reasons why the USA would wish to share the burden of Pax Americana, and Britain would wish to participate. Primarily, as the Prime Minister has said, "When Britain and America work together on the international scene, there is little we cannot achieve."[19] US forces are themselves declining and the USA is likely to welcome regional expertise, specialist forces, and self-help by allies. The participation of allies in American actions will, by internationalising them, also lend an aura of respectability if not legitimacy. By demonstrating her readiness to contribute to peace and stability in Europe as elsewhere, Britain can help keep the US engaged as the world's "principal security manager," and help prevent the rise of isolationism in the US. Finally, by burden-sharing Britain can hope to influence and even to moderate what might otherwise be "unwelcome, unilateral, tendencies on the part of the US."[20]

Fourth, greater engagement on a world-scale increases the prospect for reciprocal co-operation in matters such as sharing intelligence and countering the proliferation of weapon systems and technology. Britain could also encourage other nations to bolster their own confidence-building measures and capabilities for peace-keeping.

Britain could also take a lead, or set an example, - an ethical foreign policy would indicate she should - in all forms of soft or non-traditional security interests which require international co-operation such as crime, terrorism, drug trafficking, flight of refugees, resource shortages, and environmental decay.

Taken together these are powerful reasons why Britain needs to develop a coherent and workable, global foreign policy and a military strategy to match.

Continental and Maritime Strategies

The military strategy in which Britain has been engaged since the early years of century is a continental strategy in Europe, a strategy which has involved large-scale fighting and stationing of troops on the European mainland for most of the 20th century. This continental strategy has been an aberration in British history, an aberration which was pointed out at its inception and which Basil Liddell Hart vehemently criticised in the interwar years. "For the first time in our history," he told the Royal United Services Institute in 1931, "We poured the nation into the army."[21] Now without a continental enemy, it is appropriate to review this continental strategy. Clearly, even without the British government's determinations to conduct a Strategic Defence Review and that this review should be driven by foreign policy, a fresh strategy is needed to meet the challenges of the new world order. One of Liddell Hart's arguments was that the British way in warfare was to avoid continental military expeditions and to use maritime forces to destroy trade and to capture enemy territory. In previous centuries this was a demonstrably successful way in warfare which had enabled a small island state to grow into a world power. Today's rather more enlightened aim of such a strategy would be to help preserve peace and order in the world and to maintain stable conditions for free trade in all its forms.

Such a strategy is a maritime or expeditionary strategy, but it is necessary to be clear what is not meant by this. It does not mean the offensive strategy which originated in the USA in the 1970s and 80s as a means of waging war upon the former Soviet Union.[22, 23] The US Maritime Strategy, to give it its full title and distinguishing capital letters, was a strategy optimised for general war against the Soviet Union.[24] Nor does it mean an exclusively naval strategy in the way that those who crudely paraphrased the theories[25] of Captain Alfred Mahan, in the years preceding World War I, thought about sea power as being only about decisive battles, "der Tag," between opposing fleets. Nor does this maritime strategy equate to sea power in the sense which Stephen Roskill wrote about it after World War Two.[26] Nor even does it mean something which is in any sense the alternative to a continental strategy though sometimes continental and naval strategy, land power and sea power, are presented as mutually exclusive choices, and in a sense they are because so very often the choice demands incompatible demands on scarce budgets. Maritime strategy as it is meant in this paper is maritime in the sense in which Julian S Corbett wrote "... the principles which govern a war in which the sea is a substantial factor. Naval strategy," he wrote, "Is but that part which determines the movements of fleets when maritime strategy has determined what part the fleet must playing in relation to the action of the land forces..."[27] Corbett was writing and lecturing in 1911, no doubt writing today he would have called it not maritime but expeditionary strategy: he would certainly have embraced the army, navy and air force in what today is called joint warfare.

Corbett, who taught senior officers at the Royal Navy's War College at Greenwich, went on to alarm his then students by writing:

> "...since men live upon the land and not upon the sea, great issues between nations at war have always been decided - except in the rarest of cases - by either by what your army can do against your enemy's territory and national life, or else by the fear of what the fleet makes it possible for your army to do ..."[28]

This clearly is an expeditionary strategy, encompassing joint warfare by all three British armed forces and, of course, combined warfare with allies. Such a strategy would seem particularly appropriate to Britain's circumstances today, and the kind of role for Britain which the Prime Minister seems to want to develop. The Prime Minister has said that Britain is "... a global player [which] looks outward naturally..." who needs "...strong defence ... for British influence abroad ..." and that "...we must not reduce our capacity to exercise a role on the international stage..."[29] It is therefore natural to think that he expects British armed forces to adopt a strategy and doctrine appropriate to fulfil his vision.

Continental v. Maritime States

Writers from Adam Smith to Ralf Dahrendorf have associated economic expansion of the sort witnessed today with strong, independent middle classes, representational government, rational legal systems, checks upon arbitrary rule and an expanding franchise.[30] Liberal free trade regimes have usually been maritime ones, not least because navies cannot, except in the rarest of circumstances, be used to endanger political institutions. By contrast large standing armies, which might also contain conscripts and mercenaries, can rarely be contained within the framework of a constitutional state at peace with itself.[31]

Richard Rosecrance has characterised states which follow these two broad patterns as "merchant" states and "guardian" states. [32] "Merchant" states benefit from open trading relationships and the protection of international rules against piracy, blockade, terrorism and other, more serious, hindrances. "Guardian" states may be able to take temporary advantage of being rogues, but eventually they too reach a approximate equilibrium with the rest of the world.

The last time such conditions existed in the world were when liberal ideas and free trade prospered under the umbrella of Pax Britannia and this is no coincidence. Hugh Thomas conjured up images of merchant and guardian, light and dark, which presumably Ronald Reagan's speech-writer drew on for his image of the dark forces of evil: "... the US has constructed its wealth, its nation, and its way of life on the basis of free enterprise, free commerce and the free exchange of ideas ... it is still possible to see behind a thin veil of scientific assimilation, the shade of Pericles. In Russia, the shadow is of that of Darius the Persian..."[33] Russia and other continental states, typical of Mackinder's heartlands, like Napoleonic France and Wilhelmine and Hitler's Germany have tended to be despotic, centralising, illiberal states where the uniqueness of the individual was set at nothing. States with a maritime character seem by contrast to be free, out-ward looking, democratic, and innovative - pretty much the character of the state which Prime Minister Tony Blair has said that he aspires to lead.

Towards an Appropriate Strategy

The state must define its defence policy by three criteria: physical security of the homeland, protection of overseas possessions, and acceptable cost. Clearly in the modern world interests must be substituted for possessions. But even the USA had to deliver its strategy for defeating the Soviet Union in the Cold War by making best possible use of an affordable level of forces.[34] Policies which place an unacceptable cost in social, economic and financial terms on resources are simply not sustainable.[35]

One of the possible outcomes of the Strategic Defence Review is a defence strategy which is more expeditionary in character. This would be inherently joint in nature, drawing upon forces from all three services, both land-based and sea-based, supported by national and commercial resources, and exercising influence over land, sea and air environments.[36] Navies are already the forces which most combine the elements of joint warfare, though they may yet need to become more all-purpose.[37] The Royal Navy operates ships on and under the sea, and besides the 6,000 mile range *Trident* will soon have in service the 1,000 mile range *Tomahawk* land attack missile. The Navy also operates helicopters and fixed wing aircraft and, of course, there are some 7,000 Royal Marines who represent about 15% of the Navy's manpower. These Royal Marines, and their specialist amphibious shipping, are already at the core of Britain's Joint Rapid Reaction Force which was set up in 1996. Although a combined arms corps like the US Marine Corps (USMC) at 170,000 is as big as the Royal Navy and British Army together, it is unlikely that this or any future Defence review will produce a single self-sufficient corps like the US marines. However, the USMC and the Royal Navy's existing expeditionary capability are good models from which to start, and it is therefore appropriate to look at the doctrine of maritime strategy and the characteristics of maritime forces.

Maritime Doctrine

British armed forces are not exempted from the laws of Clausewitz: they are tools of policy intended and designed to protect and to promote national policy - they serve no other purpose. In pursuit of national policy, British Defence Doctrine sets many different scenarios in which the armed forces of the states might be used. British maritime doctrine usefully lists these in three categories: military, constabulary and benign.[38]

First, the military application of maritime force is that which uses or threatens violence, for the purposes of sea control or power projection, from long range deterrence (the strategic nuclear deterrent), operations against the land or support of forces ashore, amphibious operations which maybe used to insert or to evacuate troops or civilians, support of diplomacy, and, of course, operations in protection of trade.[39]

Second, constabulary operations are those which are needed to enforce law and order at sea, including embargo operations, sanctions, peacekeeping, anti-piracy, anti-drug and fishery protection operations, and maritime counter terrorism.[40]

Finally, benign applications of maritime force include humanitarian operations and disaster relief, search and rescue, salvage, ordnance disposal. hydrography, and assistance to the maritime community including those who live on the shore.[41]

The Characteristics of Maritime Forces

The characteristics of maritime forces are mobility, versatility, reach, lift, poise, and leverage.

Mobility is defined in British Defence Doctrine as the quality of capability of military forces to move from place to place while retaining the ability to fulfil their primary mission. Mobility provides the commander with the means of concentrating optimum force at the right time and place in a way which offers the maximum possibility to create and exploit opportunity in the battlespace.[42] Mobility is a quality which more than anything characterises a maritime strategy. Maritime forces can be deployed anywhere across the world, through contiguous seas and adjacent to 80% of the world's nations. Using missiles and aircraft maritime force can be projected far inland. Maritime forces can be deployed from Portsmouth to the coast off Pyonyang without crossing an international border.

Versatility adds to the mobility of maritime forces. The posture of maritime forces can be changed with ease, either several tasks can be conducted concurrently or new tasks adopted rapidly. Ships do not require "re-roling" in order to deploy on different missions. Each ship is a "golfbag," capable one day of conducting high intensity operations or the next of acting in a purely diplomatic role. The combination of mobility and versatility means that maritime forces can offer a wide range of flexible and well calibrated signals. The 1997 deployment of HMS *Invincible* from the Caribbean to the Gulf and the deployment of Royal Air Force's GR7 *Harrier* aircraft onboard is in example of both mobility and versatility.

Reach describes how maritime forces are in large degree autonomous, with integral logistic support which might include, for example, a full range repair and medical facilities. They have the ability to operate for extended periods and considerable distance from shore support and independent of host-nation-support. The Falklands War in 1982 when British land, sea and air forces operated at 8,000 miles remove from their UK bases is an example of reach. This reach is augmented by tankers and supply ships, and roulement means that maritime forces can be keep on station indefinitely. Examples of sustained reach are the semi-permanent presence of a frigate in the Gulf since 1980, of forces in the South Atlantic since 1982, and of an aircraft carrier for three years in the Adriatic Gulf during the crisis in the former Yugoslavia.

A significant attribute, when maritime forces are used for entry into a theatre of operations is their capacity for heavy lift. This lift may be provided by specialist amphibious shipping, by organic support vessels which will usually be fleet auxiliaries, or it may be provided by merchant shipping taken up from trade. The volume of equipment, ammunition and stores which can only go by sea, like all the main battles tanks to the Gulf War, has already been mentioned. However, it should be noted that commentators on the Strategic Defence Review have marked that British armed forces seem to lack sufficient sea and air lift capacity if they are to adopt a more expeditionary role.

Poise is used to describe the ability of maritime forces to remain in international waters and to avoid the political complications and military risks of deploying on land. They can remain for long periods poised , covertly or overtly, with or without a concerted publicity campaign, able to lend weight to diplomatic activity or to use lethal violence against the shore. Alternatively, they can be withdrawn in manner which neither conveys defeat nor climb-down. This is a unique contribution which can be used to match the pace and tone of diplomatic activity, and is particularly useful in confused and uncertain situations.

Leverage

Security is of course the sum of many functions. Clearly the greatest security comes from what Secretary of State George Robertson has called the "disarmament of the mind," which must include both preventive diplomacy and defence diplomacy.[43] Robertson calls demilitarisation of relations between its members one of NATO's great achievements, and defence diplomacy is the process and effect of military personnel meeting, talking and co-operating. "Better," he says, "to send middle aged men abroad to bore each other, than send young men to kill each other."[44] In other words, measures to build confidence between nations, and particularly between their military personnel.

However, Clausewitz's dictum must always be borne in mind that "war is ... a continuation of political intercourse, carried on with other means..."[45] Once the Clausewitzian step from diplomacy to war has been taken, a maritime strategy provides what Colin Gray has called the leverage of sea power.[46] This means that forces deployed in a maritime strategy can use the manoeuvre warfare[47] approach and create an effect on land that is disproportionate to the maritime force which is deployed. Leverage is both a strategic and an operational concept, endowed with political and military usefulness.

Leverage can be used to deter or to coerce as part of a diplomatic process, and at the operational and tactical level it can be used to strike at an enemy's critical vulnerabilities.

Maritime Manoeuvre

There is, of course, a relationship between time and space in logistics, operations and political terms.[48] With the end of the Cold War and the absence of threat at the grand strategic level there is a much reduced need for the forward deployment of forces and their equipment. This means that Britain has the logistic time and space to prepare for military operations. The absence of a grand strategic threat implies that future operations will be expeditionary and be conducted by forces of which only a part need be held at high states of readiness: they do not need to be pre-deployed

The doctrine and characteristics of maritime forces described above add up to maritime manoeuvre. Maritime manoeuvre is the ability to project military capability, including fully integrated sea, land and air forces, from the sea into those areas which are of interest to Britain, as well as to her friends and partners. In maritime manoeuvre, maritime forces optimise their inherent and enduring characteristics, use the sea as an unhindered highway, and apply force or threaten the use of force, at the time and place of political choice. Typically such force would be under a unified command (i.e. one which contains senior command elements of all three service under a single commander), structured around an aircraft carrier which would have onboard a tailored air group (i.e. the choice and mix of aircraft could be altered to suit the circumstances), reinforced with under-water launched cruise missiles, and would exploit an evolving concept of amphibious operations. The sea-basing of these forces and of essential supporting services will reduce the risk inherent in intervention operations whatever the level of conflict. Sea-basing might even eliminate altogether the need for host-nation-support.

Maritime manoeuvre is a balanced capability which would provide enough power and flexibility to ensure a measure of control of the sea and of the air while the battle or operational space is exploited.[49]

Summary

Given the above qualities, it is clear that maritime forces are uniquely suited to an expeditionary strategy. It is appropriate to summarise this chapter by quoting the judgement of Christopher Bellamy, former British army officer, former Defence correspondent of *The Independent*, and now a lecturer at Cranfield university. In his latest book, *White Knights in Armour*, he has developed a new theory of peace and war in which he concludes:

"As the new century approaches, navies are beginning to look increasingly attractive. Many of the new technologies which are likely to evolve - laser and beam weapons, for example - require enormous power which is more easily generated and transported on a ship than any other way. Navies possess unique freedom of movement, and operate at a unique state of readiness. As Mahan explained, they bridge the gap between peace and war - the very dilemma which modern strategists face. They can poise, threaten and, if necessary, attack targets increasingly far inland and put highly trained forces ashore. And they take all their supplies with them. Our preoccupation with large land armies has been very much a function of the particular problems of European security over the last two centuries ... The new century is likely to see a revival of maritime forces and of maritime strategy."[50]

The Strategy of Choice

In 1990 Eric Grove was one of the first commentators to mark that maritime forces "...have less to fear from the new world of reduced East-West tension than other forces ..."[51] Grove prophesied that it would be outside Europe that the primary potential applications of force would emerge in the future, and that, if, for example, national interests were threatened or ships carrying vital cargoes were attacked, then maritime force would be the apposite force. It is not surprising therefore that a maritime strategy (in Corbett's words), today also known as expeditionary strategy (or what Grove calls "the big E word"), is indeed likely to arise out of the government's Strategic Defence Review. As Michael Clarke of the Centre for Defence Studies at King's College, London has written, maritime forces have the most to gain from the foreign-policy approach of the

SDR. Maritime forces, he continues, will be crucial to any defence policy that seeks to serve broader international objectives.[52] Similar sentiments have been expressed in the latest issue of *Strategic Comments* from the International Institute of Strategic Studies.

In 1983 Sir James Cable wrote that "...a more maritime alignment of British strategy ... should lead to a defence posture more easily adapted to any modified foreign policy ... even if no change in foreign policy is contemplated, a predominantly maritime strategy would give [the] British government more control over their own forces and thus more political freedom of manoeuvre in a crisis ..."[53] This point is even more valid today. An expeditionary strategy, and the maritime forces which this implies, offer the country a versatile tool for diplomacy and defence appropriate to the new world order. Such a strategy would give Britain flexibility in the use of force and wide range of choice in decision-making about whether or not to intervene in any given crisis, and how to signal concern or commitment without unnecessarily risking her people by putting them ashore. Highly capable maritime forces, in addition to being major contributors to an expeditionary strategy, can also be used in a wide range of less intensive peace support operations. These qualities and capabilities are particularly suitable in the unpredictable and confused situations which might threaten either Britain's direct interests or her more altruistic ones. An expeditionary, maritime force is thus a thoroughly modern force in the modern world, offering a high level of strategic choice.

1 Robertson, George (1997): *Debate on Defence Policy*. Hansard (27 Oct).

2 Reid, John (1997): *Debate on Defence Policy*. Hansard (28 Oct).

3 Abbott, Sir Peter (1996): The Maritime Component of British and Allied Military Strategy. Royal United Services Institute Journal, December, pp. 6-11.

4 Rosecrance, Richard (1997): *Transnationalism and the Nation State. In: Security Through NATO in the 21st Century: vision to reality* in. Proceedings of a conference hosted by SACLANT and RUSI, London.

5 Politi, Alessandro (1997): *European Security: the new transnational risks.* (Chaillot Papers, 29.) Institute for Security Studies (WEU), Paris. pp. 35-8.

6 'The World Economy', *The Economist*, 20 Sep 97, p. 2.

7 Stares, Paul; Regaud, Nicolas (1997): *Europe's Role in Asia-Pacific Security*. In: Survival. (The IISS Quarterly, Winter 1997-8.) Oxford University Press, Oxford, 117-39.

8 Blair, Tony (1997): *The Principles of a Modern British Foreign Policy*. Speech by the Prime Minister at the Lord Mayor's Banquet (10 November).

9 Mahan, AT (1890): *The Influence of Sea Power upon History, 1660-1783*. Sampson Low, Marston & Co, London. p. 25.

10 Robertson, George (1997): *Debate on Defence Policy*. Hansard (27 Oct)

11 Walker, Martin (1997): *So It's Bye Bye American Pie*. The Guardian (1 Sep) .

12 Blair (1997) *The Principles of a Modern Foreign Policy*.

13 Wylie, JC (1967): *Military Strategy*. Classics of Sea Power ed. United States Institute Press, Annapolis, Md. p. 105.

14 Reid, John (1997): *Debate on Defence Policy*. Hansard (28 Oct)

15 Melrose, Diana (1997): *Submission by OXFAM to the Secretary of State for Defence on the Strategic Defence Review.* letter dated 31 Jul. (N)

16 Robertson, George (1997): *NATO, its Partners and Defence Diplomacy*. Speech by the Secretary of State to the European Atlantic Group (29 October).

17 Edmonds, Martin (1997): *Maritime Manoeuvre: expeditionary warfare, jointery and the role of the carrier.* (Bailrigg Memorandum, 28.) Centre for Defence and International Security Studies, Lancaster. p. 7.

18 Stares, &c (1997) *Europe's Role in Asia-Pacific Security*: pp 117-39.

19 Blair (1997) *The Principles of a Modern Foreign Policy.*

20 Stares, &c (1997) *Europe's Role in Asia-Pacific Security.*

21 Liddell Hart, BH (1931): *Economic Pressure of Continental Victories*, (Royal United Services Institute; 28 January; N).

22 Fraser, Stewart (1997): *US Maritime Strategy: issues and implications.* Bailrigg Paper ed. Vol. 25. Centre for Defence and International Security Studies, Lancaster. pp. 51-54.

23 Baer, George W (1994): *The US Navy, 1890-1990: one hundred years of sea power.* Stanford IUP, Stanford, Ca. pp. 428-44.

24 Friedman, Norman (1988): *The US Maritime Strategy.* Jane's, London. pp. 4-5.

25 Kennedy, Paul M (1989): *The Relevance of the Pre-war British and American Maritime Strategies to the First World War and its Aftermath, 1898-1920.* In: Maritime Strategy and the Balance of Power. (Eds: Hattendorf, John B; Jordan, Robert S) Macmillan, Oxford, p. 171.

26 Roskill, Stephen W (1962): *The Strategy of Sea Power: its application and development.* Collins, London.

27 Corbett, Julian S (1911): *Some Principles of Maritime Strategy.* Classics of Sea Power ed. (Series Ed: Grove, Eric J.) Naval Institute Press, Annapolis, Md. p. 15.

28 Corbett, *Some Principles,* p. 16.

29 Blair, Tony (1997): *The Principles of a Modern British Foreign Policy.* Speech by the Prime Minister at the Lord Mayor's Banquet (10 November).

30 Downing, Brian M (1992): *The Military Revolution and Political Change: origins of democracy & autocracy in early Europe.* Princeton UP, Princeton, NJ. p. 7.

31 Downing, p. 253.

32 Rosecrance, Richard (1997): *Transnationalism and the Nation State.* In: Security Through NATO in the 21st Century: vision to reality. Proceedings of a conference hosted by SACLANT and RUSI, London.

33 Thomas, Hugh *An Unfinished History of the World* (London: Hamish Hamilton Ltd, 1979). P. 511-6.

34 Friedman, Norman (1988): *The US Maritime Strategy.* Jane's, London. p. 5.

35 French, David (1990): *The British Way in Warfare 1688-2000*. Unwin Hyman, London. p. xi.

36 Anon. (1997): *British Defence Doctrine*. Ministry of Defence, London. pp. 13-4.

37 Clarke, Michael (1997): *Adapting to the Real Challenge*. In: Defence Review. (Ed: Langdon, Julia) Westminster Publications Ltd, London, 8-9.

38 Anon. (1997): *The Fundamentals of British Maritime Doctrine*. pp. 82-101.

39 *Fundamentals*. pp. 82-101.

40 *Fundamentals*. pp. 101-2.

41 *Fundamentals*. pp. 102-4.

42 *Defence Doctrine*. p. 6.22.

43 Robertson, George (1997): *NATO for a New Generation*. Speech at the Fifth Annual Meeting of the Atlantic Council, 19 Nov.

44 Robertson (1997) *NATO, its Partners and Defence Diplomacy*.

45 Clausewitz, Carl von (1832): *On War*. 1989 ed. (Eds: Howard, Michael; Paret, Peter.) Princeton UP, Princeton, NJ. pp. 86-7.

46 Gray, Colin S (1992): *The Leverage of Sea Power*. The Free Press, New York.

47 For the military definition of these and following words see: *The Fundamentals of British Maritime Doctrine* (London: HMSO, 1995).

48 Fry, Robert (1995): *Operations in a Changed Strategic Environment*. Royal United Services Institute June, 33-36.

49 Anon. (1997): *United Kingdom Doctrine for Joint and Multinational Operations (UKOPSDOC)*. Fourth study draft ed. Permanent Joint Headquarters, Northwood. pp. 2A-2.

50 Bellamy, Christopher (1997): *Knights in White Armour: the new art of war and peace*. Pimlico, London. p. 236.

51 Grove, Eric J (1990): *Maritime Strategy and European Security*. Common Security Studies, Brassey's, London, p. 88.

52 Clarke, Michael (1997): *Adapting to the Real Challenge*. In: Defence Review. (Ed: Langdon, Julia) Westminster Publications Ltd, London, pp. 8-9.

53 Cable, Sir James (1983): *Britain's Naval Future*. Macmillan, London. pp. 186-7.

Principles of Maritime Strategy

Eric Grove

If sea power is to be used purposefully then it must be through the application of maritime strategy. This can be defined as the art of directing maritime assets – ie those that operate on, over , or under the sea – to achieve the required political objectives. Maritime strategy involves military operations in which the sea is a principal – but not the only – factor. As Sir Julian Corbett pointed out, since people live ashore and not at sea:

> "great issues between nations at war have always been decided – except in the rarest of cases – either by what your army can do against your enemy's territory or else by the fear of what it is possible for your army to do." *Some Principles of Maritime Strategy* (1911)

Hence his insistence on the term 'maritime' rather than 'naval'. It cannot be stressed too much that *maritime* strategy *by definition* is joint in nature.

Traditionally the essence of maritime strategy has been "command of the sea". This has been best defined by Professor Geoffrey Till:

> "Being 'in command of the sea' simply means that a navy in that happy position can exert more control over the use of the sea than can any other. The degree of command varies greatly and is primarily illustrated by the extent to which it confers the capacity to use the sea for one's own purposes and to prevent the enemy using it for his." *Maritime Strategy and the Nuclear Age (1982)*

Corbett flatly stated that:

> "the object of naval warfare must always be directly or indirectly either to secure command of the sea or to prevent the enemy securing it."

In recent years the proliferation of means of denying command, the submarine, the aircraft and the increasingly powerful weapons they carry, together with the difficulty defeating them to the extent that they cannot pose serious opposition somewhere, has led to the term "command of the sea" becoming somewhat unfashionable. It has been replaced by the more limited concept of "sea control", developed at the US Naval War College in the 1970s. The term was introduced in an article in the March–April 1974 issue of *Naval War College Review* on "Missions of the US Navy" signed by Admiral Stansfield Turner:

> "The new term 'Sea Control' is intended to connote more realistic control in limited areas and for limited periods of time. It is conceivable today to temporarily exert air, submarine and surface control in an area while moving ships into position to project power or to re-supply overseas forces. It is no longer conceivable, except in the most limited sense, to totally control the seas for one's own use or to totally deny them to an enemy."

British maritime doctrine (*BR1806*) defines sea control as:

> "the condition in which one has freedom of action to use the sea for one's own purposes in specified areas and for specified periods of time."

This implies the ability to deny passage on, over and under the sea to one's opponents in the area concerned, but the essence of sea control is the proactive ability to move one's own shipping military or civil.

A major fruit of sea control is the ability to deploy surface forces to interdict the passage of the enemy's shipping using techniques such as stopping, boarding and either capturing or diverting. In war this is known as blockade but it can be used in situations short of hostilities as an embargo on certain materials and goods. Blockades and embargos can be effective, depending on the sea dependence of the target.

Sea denial is the other side of the coin to sea control. It covers attempts to stop the enemy using the sea without wishing to use it oneself for the movement of shipping. A classic form of sea denial is the *guerre de course*, a direct campaign against merchant shipping to exert economic pressure on an opponent. This kind of warfare always had some impact but it became even more important this century with the use of the submarine as its primary weapon. German U-boats twice came close to denying the United Kingdom the use of the Western approaches and US submarines massacred Japanese merchant ships.

To achieve sea control in a combat situation one needs to be able to defeat or neutralise the sea denial forces the enemy can deploy. First the enemy's main striking forces must be addressed. Up until about 1940 these striking forces were large, gun-armed capital ships whose only safe counter was one in kind. The advent of aircraft and submarines capable of inflicting decisive damage on these assets at sea undermined the supremacy of the big gun and these platforms supplanted the older capital ship as the primary naval striking arms. The new capital ships became the large aircraft carriers and the nuclear powered attack submarines of the 1950s and later, although land based strike aviation, when properly equipped for use against maritime targets, could also form a powerful component of a latter-day battlefleet, notably that of the Soviet Union during the Cold War.

The most effective means of dealing with the main enemy striking forces is to meet and defeat them in battle. This was often difficult to achieve as the inferior fleet would often maintain itself as a "fleet in being", its very existence creating risks for an opponent that tied down important assets that could have been used for other purposes. On the other hand such containment of enemy forces has the effect of covering one's own assets which can be directly protected by a lower scale of force than might otherwise be necessary. In the late Twentieth Century nuclear powered submarines provided an excellent means of containing enemy main forces. In the Falklands War HMS *Conqueror*'s sinking of the cruiser *Belgrano* made it too risky for the Argentines to risk surface battle groups against the British forces. And if there had been a major super power confrontation in the 1980s one would have seen NATO SSNs advancing to threaten Soviet ballistic missile submarines (SSBNs) in their defended "bastions" close to the USSR. This would have forced the Soviets to hold back their own SSNs to defend the SSBNs. British Maritime Doctrine calls this "containment by distraction".

The best way of dealing decisively with the air threat is to draw it out and destroy it. Aircraft have the disadvantage that they must close their targets to be effective and this forces them to give battle. The US/NATO forward maritime strategy of the 1980s was designed to bring out the Soviet Naval air arm so that the US carrier battle groups could shoot it out of the sky. The fighters carried in the carriers and the surface to air missiles of the escorts were not defensive – they were vital offensive anti-air warfare systems. Similarly, with the Argentines reduced to using shore based aircraft to interfere with the British recapture of East Falklands the missile equipped *Sea Harriers* of the two British carriers and the other Anti-Aircraft Weapons (AAW) of the carrier task group were able to defeat the enemy air forces sufficiently for the landings to take place and operations to be brought to a successful conclusion.

In the latter case, part of the attrition on the enemy was inflicted in the direct vicinity of the mission essential amphibious ships. One feature of modern naval warfare is the greater importance of escort operations, given the difficulties of containing *all* the enemy's assets or destroying them in their bases that might be heavily defended – or politically off limits. As well as engaging in operations against the enemy's major striking forces therefore there is no alternative but to deploy assets close to those one is trying to protect. Sometimes these forces play the key offensive role. In the Battle of the Atlantic in World War Two it was primarily the attrition inflicted on the U-boats around the Allied convoys that defeated the German submarine offensive against shipping. Convoy also lowered shipping losses decisively; the famous U-boat aces of the war made their reputations against unescorted shipping. The strategic lesson of history could not be clearer; shipping at risk from attack is left to sail alone at its great peril. The modern escort ship, effectively a small cruiser descended from the destroyers and frigates of the recent past, is now the basic surface combatant. Just like the cruisers of old, however, these escorts must be covered from attack that might overwhelm them by "battlefleet" assets of some kind (as the British Home Fleet generally covered the convoys from German major surface units in World War Two). It is this synergy that lies at the heart of any sea control strategy.

Once sea control is achieved, either by a campaign or because the enemy has no effective sea denial assets, then power projection against the shore can be undertaken. The ability of naval forces to directly affect operations ashore has waxed and waned over the years. The century began with the balance of advantage swinging against navies but the trend from World War Two onwards has been very much the other way. Amphibious technology and doctrine has greatly developed. The helicopter, tilt rotor and air cushion vehicle have wrought revolutions in amphibious techniques. Amphibious forces can be used for assaults, raids, demonstrations, feints or withdrawals/ evacuations. As for the shore bombardment role, the carrier borne aircraft and land attack cruise missile have allowed navies to strike effectively many hundred of miles inland. The submarine launched ballistic missile is the most effective instrument of strategic nuclear air power.

Poising afloat in an international environment, power projection forces can greatly increase the contingency options available to decision makers working in an unsure environment in a wide range of conflict and potential conflict situations, They also keep enemies guessing, tying down a disproportionate number of enemy forces in defending a coastline, rendering them unavailable for other operations.

The other side of the coin of power projection is coastal defence, a form of sea denial. Coast defence can be economically carried out by laying minefields and preventing their being swept by covering them with anti-ship missiles, carried in mobile land launchers, on fixed or rotary winged aircraft or on fast attack craft. This threat makes the use of mine countermeasures (MCM) assets difficult. The threat of Iraqi missile boats had to be eradicated before MCM operations could safely take place off Iraq in 1991. The strength of Iraqi defences prevented amphibious forces being able to play more than a distractive role, but that was not without very useful effect. Mines can also be used as general sea denial assets to close ports or other sea routes.

Coping with the mine threat is even more important now navies see themselves as operating primarily in a littoral environment, the area from open ocean to the shore, which must be controlled to support operations ashore, and the area inland from shore that can be supported and defended from the sea. Modern information technologies are allowing this environment to be networked in a true multi-dimensional maritime battlespace, with 'battlespace dominance' supplanting mere sea control as the primary aim of maritime forces. This battlespace could be very extensive allowing the advantages of the sea as a medium for the transport to allow the flexible deployment of land attack and anti-air (including anti-missile) assets that could cover forces some way inland.

Maritime power is not limited to situations where fighting has broken out. It is often at its most useful in situations short of open hostilities. There is a long tradition of "gunboat diplomacy" defined by it leading analyst, Sir James Cable as:

> "...the use or threat of limited naval force, otherwise than as an act of war, in order to secure advantage or to avert loss, either in the furtherance of an international dispute or else against foreign within the territory or jurisdiction of their own state." *[Gunboat Diplomacy 1919-91 (1994)]*

Naval forces can poise, as noted above, with minimum diplomatic preparation at an early stage in a crisis. If required they can withdraw with less embarrassment than forces deployed ashore. In short, they can maintain presence without occupation.

Maritime power has a unique combination of attributes. It operates in the medium that covers over two thirds of the world's surface and which gives access at a range of no more than a hundred miles to a similar proportion of the world's population. Maritime strategy exploits these attributes to achieve political objectives. The ability to execute a maritime strategy – one that must by definition be joint but rests on an ability to operate on, over, under and from the sea – is therefore one of a nation's most useful and powerful assets, especially if that nation is surrounded by the ocean.

The Leverage of Sea Power

Colin Gray

Sea power did not win the war [World War II] itself; it enabled the war to be won.

Herbert Richmond, *Statesmen and Seapower* (1946)

In modern times, sea power has enabled wars to be won. In ancient and medieval times, dominant land power generated the sea power that enabled wars to be won. The twentieth century has witnessed the strategic condition wherein air power, in support of sea and land power, has become a critical enabler of victory. More recently, nuclear deterrence, when appropriate, has functioned to enable conventional forces to be effective as threat and in action. For further complication, today and for the future, space power has become vital to sea power,[1] as it has to land power and air power also. War is a team enterprise. No matter how fashions in doctrine and military organisation have evolved, the historical reality has been one of joint, if frequently ill-combined – land-sea or sea-land – effort in the quest for strategic advantage. Great sea powers have required a land power dimension to their strategy, and great land powers typically have discovered that without a strong navy or naval allies, everything that they thought they had secured on land could be menaced by unreachable foes offshore with the time to make mischief.

The leverage of sea power writ large, and the strategic advantage conferred more narrowly by a superior navy, are relative to other forms of military power. Each form has a distinctive strategic utility. There are tasks that a first-class navy is good at performing, just as there are tasks that it performs either badly or not at all. In recognition of the practical necessity for a joint approach to war, as well as for more parochial reasons of service advantage, it is stunningly noticeable just how inclusive and expansive a great navy can become. The US Navy, for the leading example, in addition to its surface and sub-surface combat and support ships (and boats), also accommodates

32

a small army in the Marine Corps, and a medium-sized air force on its carriers and on naval air stations, and it operates the largest element in the strategic nuclear forces in the form of the nuclear-powered ballistic missile submarine (SSBN) fleet. As if that were not comprehensive enough, the US Navy is claiming that sea power must include space power, and, in fact, it is the largest user among the services of space systems.

For reasons of geopolitics, the major wars of the Western world in modern times typically have been conflicts characterised by large geostrategic asymmetries between the principal antagonists. Even in the rare cases when war at sea has been of equal strategic salience to both sides, the more maritime-oriented state inevitably has had a great deal more to lose at sea than has the continental foe. A case in point is the Anglo-French War of 1778–83. The unusual superficial symmetry of this war, the substantially maritime character of the struggle, was the product of the facts that Britain was tied down in a continental war an ocean away from its home base of strength, while France had assembled a united continental European front.

Wars between maritime and continental states or coalitions cannot usefully be dissected for precise determination of the relative importance of sea power or land power. A military literature which solemnly discusses the less-than-riveting issue of whether sea power, land power, air power, or economic warfare was or was not truly decisive in a particular war trivialises its subject. Any number of factors can be argued to have been decisive, in the sense that victory would not have been gained in their absence. For example, although the German Army had to be beaten in the field in World War II because the political structure of the conflict precluded a compromise peace, if unaided strategically by the Anglo-American siege of Hitler's *Festung Europa*, Soviet land power almost certainly could not have beaten the Germans. That Anglo-American siege necessarily was maritime in character, though it was a siege, and then a forcible irruption on land, utterly dependent on command of the air. What then truly was decisive or most decisive?

After the defeat of Austria at Marengo and Hohenlinden in 1800 and again after the defeat of Russia at Friedland in 1807, France decisively, indeed repeatedly, won the war on land. Hitler was in a similar favourable condition by mid-June 1940. In the British case in war after war, she won whatever there was to win at or from the sea. Enemy and enemy-leaning neutral fleets were either sunk or contained by blockade, while enemy commerce was sunk, captured, and driven from the high seas. But to achieve success in war as a whole, the centre of gravity of the foe has to be assailed convincingly. Neither sea power nor land power can be considered separately as instruments of decision in war, even with reference to a maritime-organized continental challenge to land power or a continental-based maritime challenge to sea power. Virtually by definition a great continental power can be overthrown only on land, and a great maritime power can be overthrown only at sea. But the land power that could write *finis* to a French or German Empire, or the sea power that might have terminated the maritime empires of Venice or Britain, was, or would have been, power exerted in one environment that derived its strength primarily from the other – with the *caveat* that sea power cannot be independent of material strength ashore.

Many generalizations about the importance of sea power transpire to be misleading half-truths, or truths from only one strategic perspective. It is essential to specify whether a particular claim about the significance of sea power – for example, its effect on the duration of a war – pertains to maritime effort by or against a continental state or coalition. The influence of success by a continental power on land or on the sea, and of similar success by a maritime power, requires careful treatment. For example, the influence of land power upon sea campaigns is, at least in part, strategic in nature. The course and outcome of combat on land will determine the geostrategic terms of reference of conflict at sea, as well as the balance of resources that a continental power is at liberty to devote to maritime campaigns. Also, a sea power lives or dies by its maritime communications, but obviously not literally at sea. Defeat at sea, or even a condition of severely contested command, will have a much shorter audit trail to comprehensive national defeat for a sea power than is the case for a land power beaten afloat, but the effect may still be indirect. Actual military defeat – the loss of command through a naval disaster – will lead a sea power to anticipate conquest by invasion or, perhaps, a maritime blockade which would cause an intolerable depression of economic activity.

Preponderant continental power can function strategically for the intended ultimate humbling of insular sea power. Because land power can achieve decision on and against the national territory of its enemies in a way that sea power cannot, it does not follow that it is more strategic in character than is sea power. When confronted with the barrier of a sea commanded by the enemy, land power ceases to be an instrument of military decision by the enemy. One argument is that modern history has shown the inability of preponderant continental powers to fashion potent enough maritime (or air) instruments for the defeat of insular sea powers. Another, more convincing, is that no land power has been sufficiently preponderant on land as to have the surplus resources necessary for the conduct of successful war against insular great-power enemies.

Sea power, land power, and air power are partners rather than foes. Each needs the others if success in war is to be achieved. And they are always specific to country, strategic context, and tactical feasibility. Sea power ever is about the performance of particular missions in particular places with an actual quantity and quality of force and ancillary services, in face of a particular enemy. General analyses that purport to track comparatively the relations of net advantage as among sea power, land power, and air power may have some limited utility – for example, with reference to the evolving basics of transportation economics assessed in the currency of comparative ton-mile costs – but they can easily lead the unwary astray. In tending toward the isolation of sea power from its dependence on a particular territorial base of resources, discussion of maritime-continental strategic interaction fundamentally may fail to understand the structure of its subject. For example, the debate in the 1980s over the US maritime strategy was plagued with strategic-theoretical generalities which often obscured the fact that the sea power of the Western Alliance united, and was a partial expression of, truly gigantic landward economic resources.

Notwithstanding the vast differences of detail as among ancient, medieval and modern times, there has been a sufficient continuity in the leverage of sea power for statecraft and strategy as to lend itself to presentation as unified conclusions. Moreover, these conclusions speak as clearly to the present and the future as they do to the past.

Two general truths obtain with respect to the significance of maritime prowess for the outcomes of wars between sea powers and land powers. *First, a continental power can win a war by securing military command at sea, by achieving sea denial, or even just by disputing command at sea very vigorously.* Occasionally, traditionally continental powers have proved capable of developing or renting a quality and quantity of naval power sufficient to render the further prosecution of war impracticable for a sea power foe. Unlike land powers, sea powers can lose wars as a more or less direct consequence of defeat or damage suffered at sea. For example, courtesy of rentable maritime allies and Persian gold, Sparta discovered that the only strategy likely to bring down an already much weakened Athens was blockade of the Athenian grain supply at the choke point of the Dardanelles. For another case, in the First Punic War, the Roman Republic was sufficiently robust in public spirit, and well endowed with continental resources, that it could build and rebuild a fleet such that the maritime empire at Carthage was at a greater disadvantage in the seaward dimension of the struggle in Sicily than it was on land. In modern times, neither France nor Germany succeeded in sustaining a naval challenge to Britain to the point where Britain was obliged to sign a peace of humiliation, let alone actual surrender.

Second, for a sea power or a maritime-dependent coalition, command at sea provides the strategic conditions indispensable for success in war.

British sea power in 1914–18, Anglo-American sea power in 1939–45, and NATO's sea power in the Cold War brought the resources of virtually the whole maritime-accessible world to bear upon a continental struggle in Europe. Furthermore, as Napoleon and then Hitler discovered, an uncommanded sea places strict geographical and hence military, economic, and political limits upon what can be achieved by victorious land power. When triumphant armies reach the water's edge, they reach the limit of their military competence. The question, then, is whether continental victory can work as an enabler for success at sea. For the land power, that success need take the form only of sea denial, since the critical strategic necessity is to prevent the maritime enemy from using the sea for self-sustenance by overseas supply or for power projection against the shore.

The discussion of land power and sea power subsumes the air power most appropriate to each. World War II demonstrated conclusively, while every war since has driven the principle home further, that lasting success on the ground and at sea requires success in the air. Overall judgements on the leverage of sea power and the strategic advantage conferred by superior naval strength incorporate recognition of the roles and significance of air power, when relevant historically.

Superior sea power enables a maritime-dependent state or coalition to protract a conflict in time in pursuit of victory. For reasons of geopolitics, economic geography, and the political instability of empires, protracted conflict tends strongly, if painfully, to favour the prospects both of insular power and of continental power that has extraordinary depth. There is a centuries-long pattern of democratic, or relatively democratic, commercial-minded sea powers choosing to neglect their defenses in peacetime, riding out some military setbacks at the outset of a war, and then, with the benefit of sea control, organizing and mobilizing a materially overwhelming coalition for the overthrow or profound discouragement of an aspiring continental hegemon. In similar ways, the Dutch Republic, Britain, and the United States have all been able to rely on their own or another state's naval power to keep their homelands secure for a period of mobilization. In the late seventeenth and early eighteenth centuries, the Dutch were rendered insular to an important degree by the barrier fortresses of the Spanish (later Austrian) Netherlands and by their ability to breach their dikes at will.[2] The Channel under the working control of the Royal Navy allowed Britain to survive the disasters on land in the wars against the French Revolution and Empire, provided a totally secure flank for Anglo-French land power in 1914–18, and denied Hitler the short-war victory, or peace negotiated under severe duress, that he believed he had earned in the summer of 1940.

Given the generally tolerable congruency of British and American vital interests, save briefly late in the Napoleonic period, Britain's maritime-dependent antihegemonic policies served the United States almost as well as they did Britain itself. In earlier periods, in the face of disasters on land, the effective insularity conferred upon the citadel of the Byzantine Empire by the unbreachable Great Wall of Theodosius (until the coming of heavy siege artillery using gunpowder) that protected Constantinople on its landward side, or the long walls to Piraeus that rendered inland Athens militarily an island, enabled the sea power of Byzantium and of Athens to keep the state alive and to protract conflicts in hope of a change in strategic fortune.

It is not inevitable that time must work in favour of a dominant sea power in conflict with a dominant land power, but the structure of security politics in continental Eurasia, and the increasing economic significance of the world beyond that dual continent, makes it more likely than not that that will continue to be so. Although today it can be threatened with bombardment from the air, the world beyond the reach of armies in Eurasia can be approached only by sea.

Next, superior sea power provides a large measure of control over the geostrategic terms of engagement in war. Among the examples worth citing are the great Athenian expedition to Sicily in 415–413 B.C., Republican Rome's ability in the Second Punic War to regulate the scale and scope of war in Spain for the purpose of discouraging Carthage from reinforcing Hannibal in south-central Italy, and the English fine-tuning in the sixteenth century of the wars of attrition against Spain on the Continent that were waged in the Netherlands and in Brittany. Further cases include the "Spanish ulcer" that Britain sustained with its protracted (1808–14) Peninsular commitment, the Anglo-French extended raid to the Crimea (and the Baltic) in 1854–55,[3] Gallipoli and Salonika in the First World War, and virtually the entire Anglo-American geostrategic direction of the Second World War in Europe and the Pacific.

There is another side to this story. An enemy superior on land is certain to be able to seize continental prizes which a maritime coalition would very much like to be able to defend and will need to recapture or otherwise recover. Also, geographically eccentric axes of peripheral attack may be forced upon a sea power by the strength of enemy land power. From 1940 until 1945 the Western allies were enabled by their supremacy at sea to choose to prosecute war in North Africa, and then in Sicily and on the Italian mainland. But they were fighting in the Mediterranean because they lacked the strength to fight in the main theatre of operations: in France, the Low Countries, and beyond to Germany itself.

The continuity of the oceans means that maritime command confers a global mobility and agility with which shore-bound or even air-transportable land power cannot compete. As Halford Mackinder and others predicted around the turn of the century,[4] the coming of the railway (and subsequently the internal combustion engine), and more generally the maturing of continental-scale industrial economies, provided a strategic and tactical mobility for military forces on land that previously they had most noticeably lacked. The inability of the leaders of Britain's Royal Navy in the years leading up to 1914 to persuade anyone of note outside its ranks of the military practicality of conducting useful raids on the German coast, was evidence of the plausibility of the contemporary German view that such a threat had been long overtaken by developments in the logistics of land power.[5] Prior to that new-found political, industrial and military organization of the continents which Mackinder discerned as working to the great disadvantage of sea power, Britain reliably could wage peripheral land warfare at a logistical advantage over continental enemies. This was the case in both the Peninsula and the Crimea. The *potential* offensive value of superior sea power was demonstrated in the First World War at Gallipoli and Salonika. The hallmark of that offensive value lies in the mobility and flexibility with which sea-based force can be concentrated for surprise application. The actual benefit of the offensive use of the mobility of sea-based military power was shown on a heroic scale by the Western-Allied conduct of the Second World War in all theatres. Abstract notions pertaining to the contemporary tactical relationship between sea and land mobility were demonstrated from 1942 until 1945 to be thoroughly misleading guides to the realm of the militarily practicable. The invasions of North Africa, Sicily, Italy (including the instructive near-disaster of Salerno and the fiasco of Anzio), and France are not in any useful sense to be thought of as representational confrontations between land-based and sea-based power. Rather, the beaches of French North Africa, Sicily, Italy, and France witnessed the engagement in all dimensions of Allied and Axis military power in particular places at particular times.

The mobility of sea power translates as an inherent agility that maritime command can exploit to achieve surprise. By their nature, naval forces are manoeuvre forces. Surprise at and from the sea is facilitated by the fact that naval forces are not canalized in their axes of threat as land forces are by natural and man-made obstacles. Furthermore, the typically tenuous nature of the contact maintained between hostile naval forces at sea enhances the feasibility of surprise. It is traditional to talk of sea *lanes, highways, routes,* and *lines* of communications, but these territorial and geometric notions invite misunderstanding as to just how difficult it can be to locate ships precisely in the vast expanse of the oceans. In the summer of 1798 Nelson could only guess whither Admiral François Brueys' fleet was bound – with reference to the frustrating chase in the dark that eventually was concluded with the Battle of the Nile, after Nelson had pursued several false trails. For a further Nelsonian example, consider the Trafalgar campaign that was terminated so conclusively on October 21, 1805. The campaign opened in March with Villeneuve evading the Royal Navy's blockade of Toulon and baffling Nelson as to his destination and purpose – the eastern Mediterranean or the Atlantic? And if the Atlantic – the West Indies or Brest and the Channel?

After the fashion of the German situation in the West in 1943–44, "fortress land power" may be certain that the sea-commanding enemy is coming and can estimate the risks and benefits of each plausible axis of attack. But as the allies demonstrated even with regard to the execution of the largest amphibious assault in history (*Overlord,* June 6, 1944), the natural mobility of sea power facilitates deception for operational surprise. Deception and surprise are not uniquely characteristic of the potential of sea power, but strategic and tactical surprise tend to be easier to accomplish at and from the sea than they are on land because of the multiplicity of routes that ships, but not armies, can take. Surprise is both more feasible at sea than on land, and its tactical, and possibly strategic, benefits can be far more devastating. The fleet caught at a disadvantage typically will not have fortified places into which it can retire promptly and safely. Moreover, the small number of major combat units (compared with land warfare) in war at sea means that a handful of salvoes could overturn a particular naval balance.

Time and again superior sea power has worked strategically to knit together geographically widely separated countries for the conduct of war as a coalition enterprise. Most critical of all for eventual victory has been the role of sea power in tying together the war effort of maritime and continental states acting in concert. Oceans can connect or divide, depending upon who commands them. The wartime impact of British, then Anglo-American, sea power from 1939 to 1945 was not a matter strictly of the fighting and mercantile maritime assets of those countries, or, more broadly, of the abstract value of sea power. Instead, the subject was the naval and mercantile assets generated by the specific national economies and security communities they expressed and connected. Anglo-American sea power, with its air power adjunct, brought an armed *world* to bear against Hitler's overmatched European fortress.

In modern times, command of the sea has enabled the leading sea power to wage war of such a character on the sea and by land that the continental enemy has either retired exhausted from the contest or has been overthrown militarily. Moreover, the offshore sea power repeatedly has been able to organize, finance (and even equip), and support directly on land continental states connected by maritime strength to the seaward world controlled by superior naval power. Hegemonic land power has brought on its own arrest or destruction by the continental opposition that it cannot help but arouse.

There have been cases of continental states acquiring navies that wrested command of the sea from more natural sea powers, though not in modern times. Even if a continental naval power seeks only the negative object of denial of sea control to its maritime enemy, however, achievement of that limited object truly could be decisive. Spain, France, and Germany successively and repeatedly failed to solve the maritime problems in war-making which Britain imposed upon them. They might have succeeded. In principle, though not to date in practice, pursuit of the *guerre de course* was a sound strategy for a second-class navy. Britain's battle-fleet command and the sheer volume and distribution of value of its seaborne commerce in very many hulls defeated France in the "tonnage wars" of the antitrade campaigns of the late seventeenth, eighteenth, and early nineteenth centuries. But British experience twice in the twentieth century must suggest to the prudent that commerce raiding has the potential to defeat a sea power, a potential that was rendered dramatically actual in the Pacific war wherein US submarines on their own all but defeated the Japanese maritime empire. Whether the oceans connect an overall overmatching war machine, or whether they divide "islands" of war-making resources which cannot project their power, is a function of the ability of a maritime coalition to keep the seas secure.

The leverage of sea power works in a multifaceted *enabling* capacity. Naval strength, no matter how dominant, is rarely able by its own unaided action to exert decisive pressure upon an enemy. That is not a criticism. It is simply a fact to recognize that sea power, land power, and air power have unique and complementary capabilities. Superior sea power exerts leverage by its ability to enlist time as a critical ally and by its invaluable capacity to shape the geostrategic terms of engagement in war. By landlocking the foe, superior sea power can isolate, divert, and distract while using its inherent mobility to express a strategic and operational agility to achieve a useful measure of surprise. The landlocking of a typically impatient continental enemy encourages him to throw the dice in ever more ambitious continental adventures. A continental power frustrated strategically at the low-tide line will turn to try to maximize whatever gain his armies can secure on land. That was the strategic history of the fall of Napoleonic France and of Germany twice.

Dominant, if often challenged, sea power repeatedly has exerted the decisive economic leverage in war through its ability to bond together a materially very superior coalition of states. British, or Anglo-American, sea power connected the entire world of friendly as well as unfriendly shorelines. The former comprised a maritime network of economic strength; the latter were potential targets for the projection of military power from the sea.

The future value to statecraft and strategy of the ability to use or deny use of the seas is predictable with high confidence. The connecting and isolating value to strategy of superior sea power is a persisting fact of physical and political geography. Humankind lives on politically organized territories which more often than not are imperfectly bonded by ground or air transportation. The slowness of sea passage relative to land, air, missile or cyberspace conveyance is as unarguable as it remains inescapable, but close to irrelevant, for still critical purposes.

There are no trends extant – technological, economic, political, or military – which suggest an imminent diminution in the strategic leverage of sea power. The potency of air power certainly has improved dramatically, as witness its leading role in the Gulf War of 1991. The dominant navy of this age, however, the navy of the United States, has integrated air (breathing) power in its carriers and in its acquisition of conventionally armed cruise missiles. Furthermore, the US Navy is well launched on the process of accommodating the force-multiplying benefits of space systems and of technologies for the exploitation of cyberspace. On balance, far from threatening the strategic obsolescence of otherwise superior naval power, air and space power has made some navies unprecedentedly potent in relative terms.

Wherever and however one looks, high leverage for sea power in the future seems a certainty. On the political front, the demise of one of the superpowers eliminates for a while the most nominally persuasive of threats to the strategic utility of sea power: the peril of a war so brief and destructive that sea power's enabling action would be short-circuited by nuclear catastrophe. It is true that nuclear threats to the leverage of sea power are becoming regional or local rather than global in character, but it is also true that first-class sea power tomorrow will provide convincing antimissile, as well as antiaircraft, defences. The US Navy has shifted its principal focus from sea control to power projection against the shore and from the deep ocean to shallow water. In the absence of a plausible enemy with a first-class sea power, American maritime strategists talk of operational manoeuvre from a deep sea whose control is unlikely to be in dispute for many years to come.

The predictable continuities in physical geography, in comparative transportation economics as among geographical environments, and in the political proclivities for conflict, all argue for the enduring strategic leverage of sea power. If the coming of the railway, internal combustion engine, air, missile, nuclear, and space eras could not demote the strategic value of sea power significantly, it is difficult to see what could emerge to do so over the next several decades.

1   'The Influence of Space Power upon History', *Comparative Strategy*,
     Vol. 15, No. 4 (October–December 1996), pp. 293–308.

2   For illustration of the all but insular position of the Dutch, see
     Philippe Masson, *De la Mer et de sa stratégie* (Paris: Tallandier, 1986),
     p. 343.

3   See Andrew W. Lambert, *The Crimean War: British Grand Strategy,
     1853–56* (Manchester: Manchester University Press, 1990). Basil
     Greenhill and Ann Gifford, *The British Assault on Finland,
     1854–1855: A Forgotten Naval War* (London: Conway Maritime
     Press, 1988), also is excellent.

4   In Halford J. Mackinder, *Democratic Ideals and Reality* (New York:
     W.W. Norton, 1962), the key essay, 'The Geographical Pivot of
     History,' dates from 1904. Also see J.R. Seeley, *The Expansion of
     England* (Chicago: University of Chicago Press, 1971), ch. 7, which
     dates from 1881–82.

5   See Arthur J. Marder, *From the Dreadnought to Scapa Flow: The
     Royal Navy in the Fisher Era, 1904-1919*, vol. 1: *The Road to War,
     1904–1914* (London: Oxford University Press, 1961), pp. 386–94.

The Technology of Maritime Power

Norman Friedman

Navies offer governments two complementary virtues. One is mobility: a navy can carry heavy weapons virtually effortlessly over vast distances, and its ships can remain offshore for extended periods, unbidden by any local power. Similarly, merchant ships remain the only viable means of moving heavy cargoes over the globe; naval forces are used to protect that mobility. The other virtue is effective invisibility for ships beyond the horizon.[1] Relatively small numbers of ships have often exerted enormous power because those they threatened had to prepare against a wide variety of threats, spread over a vast area. These two virtues are exercised in a variety of ways, and their preservation calls forth a variety of technical solutions. For example, during the Cold War Soviet bombers and submarines seriously threatened naval mobility, and much of NATO's naval effort went into dealing with those threats. Much also went into insuring that NATO (particularly the US Navy) could mount the sort of credible amphibious threat that would force the Soviets to spread out their coast defences, hopefully to the point of reducing ready ground forces capable of assaulting NATO borders directly.[2]

Surface warships in particular offer a special value: they can be seen on a sustained basis. Simply by being present, they can reassure friends and threaten those who would become hostile. If hostilities begin, they can exert national power. Only a surface warship combines endurance, often in waters where it may not be particularly welcome, with visible power.[3] It is sometimes argued that the combination of satellite surveillance and improved anti-ship weapons (particularly cruise missiles) has drastically reduced the value and viability of surface warships. It seems fairer to say that continued work is necessary to ensure that surface warships remain viable and credible. To lose that viability would have wide and devastating consequences. If navies cannot maintain their warships on the surface of the sea, there is surely no great hope for the maritime trade those navies hope to protect. Similarly, there is no place for amphibious forces, which are so often the best instruments for intervention abroad. Submarines, which are sometimes advanced as the natural successors to surface ships, have vital roles; but for fundamental reasons they are unlikely to have the cargo capacity needed for trade or for amphibious operations.

As it happens, the surface ship situation is now better than it has been for some time. The only hostile power with a serious ability to conduct open-ocean surveillance is no longer a major threat. As for the missile threat, modern combinations of radar and quick-reaction defensive missiles are far better now than in the past, and improvements in computers promise to improve matters further. That is not to say that all problems have been solved, only to say that this is a happier time than, say, a decade or two earlier. Certainly the surface warship is still extremely important. The world may now lack any credible blue water threat, but it is clearly quite unstable. Navies offer their governments the ability to intervene, in a measured way, abroad; to impose pressure without the need to maintain large foreign garrisons. Too, they may offer their governments the means to deny others the full mobility of the sea. That may entail embargoes, such as those in the Adriatic or in the Gulf, or it may mean attempts to stop ships carrying illegal weapons of mass destruction.[4]

Intervention is hardly a new idea. It is now often called a littoral operation, the term emphasising concentration on what happens at or beyond another country's coastline. Littoral warfare includes both quick air attacks, such as the US strikes on Libya in 1986, and amphibious operations in which troops are landed and sustained ashore. In both cases, the enabling technology is twofold: that needed to neutralise an enemy's coastal defences, and that needed to strike targets well inland from the sea, using limited resources. Littoral warfare is more difficult than blue-water warfare because it occurs in a much more complex environment, and because an enemy has more resources close to home. Too, a fleet operating near an enemy's shore is likely to be quite observable, losing much or all of the cardinal virtue of invisibility. The main current threats to the fleet are anti-ship cruise missiles (fired by aircraft, surface craft, submarines, or from shore), torpedoes (fired mainly by enemy submarines), and mines (particularly, but not only, near the beach). A fixed amphibious objective area may also be threatened by an enemy's theatre ballistic missiles (like the Iraqi *Scuds* of the Gulf War). To make matters more complex, terrain may mask airborne attackers until too late. Similarly, underwater terrain is likely to make long-range sonar operation difficult at best.

Some interesting answers are now emerging. During the Cold War, the US Navy became interested in what it now calls the Co-operative Engagement Capability (CEC), in which several ships could share a common radar picture of such high quality that it could be used directly for fire control. The key was that all ships in the net had similar very capable *Aegis* (SPY-1) radars; too, the number of ships in the net was strictly limited (so that a very dense stream of data could be used).[5] Each ship in the net has a standard computer running standard software; in theory, then, each ship makes the same decision as to whether or not to engage a target that any ship in the CEC net detects. The computer also decides how to engage the target. CEC can now accept other weapon systems; its standard software can evaluate their capabilities, compared to those of *Aegis* ships. For example, an aircraft carrier armed with short-range defensive missiles can fire them at targets it has not yet detected, using CEC data. At present, a CEC net includes up to 24 units. It seems likely that CEC will eventually be offered to allied navies, just as all NATO navies currently share in Link 11 (a digital link between ships' combat direction systems). In a littoral situation, CEC allows a ship to engage an air target which it cannot see, as long as some other ship (or radar) in the net does see the target. That will often solve the problem presented by terrain (and also by radar propagation, which becomes more complex inshore). CEC also promises to reduce the effectiveness of some important stealth techniques. Stealth is often achieved by shaping a vehicle to reflect radar signals away from the transmitter pointed at it. In effect, CEC provides many radar receivers in different directions, at least some of which may pick up these diverted echoes. To some extent, then, it converts a fleet's radars into a single unified multi-static radar. The CEC concept, of shared sensor data and of common software to decide how to use shipboard weapons, is extremely powerful. It is likely to have two other applications. The simplest is antisubmarine. As in the case of a pre-CEC air defence ship, a ship processes her own sonar data (acoustics); she may pass the resulting datum to another ship. The only exception is that the ship may receive acoustic data from her helicopter. Now, however, at least in the United States work, is proceeding on CEC-like high-capacity underwater warfare data links. This will automatically provide a group of ships with a multi-static sonar system, which may (in effect) see around underwater obstacles, just as CEC sees around above-water terrain. Multi-statics should also help screen out many of the problems of shallow-water operation, such as extraneous noise and reflection off the bottom.[6]

The other likely near-term application of CEC concepts is to attacks on shore targets. An army coming ashore needs fire support. If the fleet offshore can provide not only short-term support, but also much of the army's artillery needs, then much less has to be landed, at least in the early phases of an operation. Any reduction in the mass of materiel which has to be landed much simplifies problems such as mine countermeasures, which are particularly serious in shallow water inshore. Against these potential advantages, modern surface navies deploy far less shore bombardment firepower than their World War II or Korean or even Vietnam War predecessors. On the other hand, some of that firepower can be used quite far inland. At present the US Navy hopes to extend 5-inch gun range out to beyond 60 miles, using rocket boosted Global Positioning System (GPS) guided shells, and there are plans for much greater ranges (shells are attractive because they take up so much less volume than missiles, hence can be carried in much greater quantities – as long as unit costs can be held down).[7] To the guns can be added special attack missiles and also carrier-based aircraft. The hope is clearly that these varied resources can do the job if only they are used more efficiently. At present, these weapons are not integrated. If the commander of an amphibious operation wants a target destroyed, he must order a specific ship to do that job; in many cases that means choosing a specific weapon. As gun and missile ranges increase, moreover, it becomes essential to ensure that outbound shells and missiles do not accidentally hit friendly aircraft, since they quickly reach aircraft-operating altitudes. Too, weapons are fired based on a manually updated map of the situation. Calls for fire must travel up through several echelons. Although the system works well enough near the beach, it is hardly flexible enough to deal with a fast moving battle inland. Yet there are vast advantages to be gained if much of the heavy firepower the troops use stays offshore. The problems are really not too far from the ones CEC and earlier forms of combat direction automation addressed: a complex tactical picture, developing too fast for manual updating, a complex array of weapons, choices among which must be made based on their capabilities, and problems of potential conflict between surface weaponry and aircraft. It helps that the US Army is trying to automate the formation of its own tactical picture. Given sufficient computer power, that tactical picture can be displayed in map form (on a computer screen or screens) aboard an amphibious flagship and fire support ships. The CEC-like goal is that the commander of the attack should be able to limit himself to selecting a target ashore, based on this tactical picture. The system should then select the optimum weapon and attack the target, making the most efficient possible use of existing resources. To the extent that the resources will be missiles, it will probably be necessary to couple the air defence and shore bombardment CECs. Most ships will be equipped with vertical launchers which can accommodate several different weapons for both purposes. The automated weapons assigners will have to know which ships are carrying which mixes of weapons, and also which weapons of each type have already been expended. Littoral warfare also carries a new type of threat from the shore: the theatre or tactical ballistic missile.

Although such weapons cannot currently attack moving ships, they certainly can strike at forces concentrated in an amphibious area just ashore. In the past, the main threats to such forces were aircraft. The expectation was that the amphibious attacker could achieve tactical surprise sufficient to preclude a land counterattack, but that defending aircraft could react quickly enough. As it was further out to sea, the solution was a mixture of defending aircraft and missiles. Clearly aircraft cannot deal with the ballistic missile threat. Missiles have a better chance. During the Gulf War, the SPY-1 radars on US missile cruisers routinely tracked Iraqi *Scud* ballistic missiles. More recently, in 1996, a US cruiser was able to track Chinese M-9 ballistic missiles fired at target areas near Taiwan. To provide earlier warning, ships can be cued by satellites (the United States deploys several infra-red satellites of the Defense Support Project [DSP] system, which cued ships and *Patriot* defensive missiles during the Gulf War). Currently the US Navy is working on a variant of its *Standard* anti-aircraft missile specifically to deal with incoming theatre ballistic weapons. Presumably ships will carry a mixture of anti-missile, anti-aircraft, and strike missiles in their vertical launch cells. There must always be a fear that the particular ship finding itself under attack by, say, air-breathing missiles will not have enough defensive weapons, that too great a variety of missiles is being demanded. The answer seems to be CEC: other ships in the group can automatically help. Advances like CEC and its ilk and new missiles are attractive partly because they can be realised at a relatively low cost in ship installation, without buying new hulls. CEC does require new and very powerful computers, but the current level of technology makes them quite compact. At least in their US form, vertical launcher cells are extremely adaptable.[8]

Mines continue to be a very difficult threat, particularly to a battle group moving far too fast to be accompanied by mine countermeasures craft. Clearing a path through a minefield is currently extremely laborious because the specialist minehunters must separately detect each mine-like object, then examine it from a safe distance (using a robot submersible), and only then destroy it, before moving on. The near-term solution appears to be a remotely-controlled mine-hunting vehicle, which can operate ahead of a battle group, transmitting back what its sonar sees by radio link. Hopefully, those on board the receiving ship can decide whether the objects seen are mines, and they can command the remote vehicle to attack them with anti-mine charges. The great advantage of the remotely-controlled vehicle is that, being unmanned, it can be risked in the midst of a potential minefield. A variation on this theme is an unmanned underwater vehicle, which can thread its way through a potential minefield. Hopefully, its own signatures are too weak to set off any of the mines. It brings its data home, and the minefield is then mapped for destruction or evasion.

Another variation is a helicopter-borne laser, which can see down well below the surface, again mapping the minefield. Again, mapping can be relatively quick because the observing device is unlikely to set off mines as it traverses the minefield. New surface warships are still, of course, being built. Several important changes are either ongoing or close to the point of adoption. First, the shapes of surface ships are changing to make them less detectable, at least to radar. The hope is not so much to build invisible ships, as to reduce the radar cross-section of a ship sufficiently for an anti-ship missile to prefer a decoy such as a chaff cloud. Current design features for greater stealth include avoidance of square corner reflectors (including the corner made by the hull as it intersects the water) and the widespread use of radar-absorbing material (RAM) on upperworks. It is possible that clever management of a ship's radar signature will tend to lead attacking missiles, if they do lock onto the ship, into relatively harmless hits at the ends rather than in the ship's vitals. Lower observability clearly extends to the ship's radiating sensors and radios. Here the main development is wide band electronics which can distribute a signal over a wide bandwidth, with very little of that signal at any particular frequency. The most striking current example is the Dutch *Scout* radar, a surface search set whose peak power is far less than a thousandth that of a conventional set. *Scout* works because radar detection range depends not on peak power, but rather on average power; on the other hand, current radar detectors depend on peak power. Whether advances in computer power can produce a new generation of detectors which can deal with the new stealthy emitters is another question.

Second, ships are gaining combat survivability through the use of survivable data busses (data highways). In the past, all of a ship's vital sensors and weapons were directly wired to the ship's central computer. Any break in that wiring would neutralise the ship. A bus, however, can be duplicated. Many ships have one running along the keel, another on one side at the waterline, and a third on the other side at deck-edge level. Individual weapons and sensors are wired, not to the central computer, but to each duplicated bus element. The step beyond, which has not generally been taken, is to spread out the computers of the ship's combat direction system, so that no single hit can claim them all. Even so, the combination of the bus and the use of multiple computers makes repair after battle damage much easier, and also makes it easier to modify a ship (much less wiring need be ripped up, and individual computers can be replaced without uprooting the whole of the ship's software).

A third trend, towards all-electric ships, is more speculative. Current ships have two separate power plants, one for propulsion and one (electric) to power the ship's systems, including her weapons and sensors. In most cases, the prime mover plant is connected to propellers via shafts. If the ship suffers shock damage, the shafts may spring, opening up the hull (as actually happened to HMS *Prince of Wales* in 1941). At the least, shafts occupy space aft which might better be used for additional weapons, for example for vertical launchers (a US *Spruance* class destroyer has no vertical launchers aft because shafts occupy the necessary space; that roughly halves the weapons capacity of the ships).

If electric motors (as in many submarines) are substituted for geared drive, then the ship's prime movers can be split up and distributed around the hull. It becomes much more difficult to stop a ship by destroying her machinery. One might even imagine adding podded motors driving propellers forward, so that a ship can survive even if her stern is blown off. Another advantage of electric drive is that the generators can be noise-mounted high up in the ship, rather than low in the ship where silencing is so difficult. The Royal Navy's Type 23 already takes advantage of this possibility in a limited way, in its quiet diesel-electric low-speed power plant (the gas turbines drive through conventional shafts).

The next step is to unify primary and auxiliary power plants, using the same turbo-generators or diesel generators for both roles. In the past, electric drive was generally resisted because the generators and motors added considerable weight and demanded much more volume. Now, apparently, electric motor-generator technology has advanced enormously. Gas turbines themselves are so light that the increased weight is affordable. The remaining obstacle is that the usage profiles for primary and auxiliary power are quite different, so that the ship must be able to switch loads rapidly. That requires a software controlled high power switchboard, which is now under development.

One advantage of the electric ship is that it is well adapted to carry a new generation of electric weapons, such as very high velocity rail guns, which show considerable promise. Much the same has been said in the past of electric lasers for close-in air defence. In either case, switching almost all power briefly to charge up a bank of capacitors would provide the ship with the power to shoot. If charge-up time were very short, the loss of propulsive power might be almost imperceptible. There is also interest in new hull forms, such as the trimaran currently under development in Britain. The logic of the new hull is that the emphasis in surface warship design has changed from an emphasis on internal volume (in smaller ships, largely to accommodate machinery) to one on deck area (to accommodate helicopters and vertical missile launchers). The change is possible because gas turbines are so much more compact than their steam turbine predecessors. It is argued that a multi-hull ship (a SWATH or a trimaran, for example) will be a far better sea-keeper than a conventional displacement hull. Whether that is true remains to be seen. For example, a displacement hull may be able to accommodate changes in load more easily than a multi-hull low water-plane design such as a trimaran. This and associated questions will probably be resolved within ten to fifteen years.[9]

1   One might read much of the development of navies in this century as
a struggle for and against effective invisibility. During World War I,
British successes in breaking German naval codes (and in using radio
direction-finding) drastically reduced the invisibility of the German
High Seas Fleet, leading to, among other things, the Battle of Jutland.
Conversely, one cardinal virtue of convoying merchant ships in all
eras was that it emptied much of the sea of ships, frustrating commerce
raiders; in other words, it enhanced the invisibility of naval targets (a
whole convoy was not so much larger than an individual ship as to
make it much easier to detect). During World War II the Germans
tried to overcome the invisibility of convoys by a combination of
code--breaking and U-boat patrol lines. They in turn lost invisibility
because the U-boat scouts had to report their findings, so that sufficient
U-boats could be concentrated to deal with the convoy and its
escorts. During the Cold War, the Soviet Union built up a system of
passive and active radar satellites specifically to detect and track
NATO naval formations – to overcome their invisibility. The active
portion of this system is no longer in service. In littoral warfare, the
range of coastal radars can be no more than a few tens of miles (to
the radar horizon), but under some conditions (ducting) it can be
several hundred miles. The recent development of high-frequency
surface-wave radar may extend the usual radar horizon to about 180
nautical miles, but few such sets have yet been sold. Maritime patrol
aircraft also extend the effective horizon, but few countries have
enough such aircraft to mount sustained surveillance.

2   The amphibious threat was an important element of the Maritime
Strategy pursued by the US Navy during the 1980s. The hope was
that the threat would dilute Soviet forces on the Central Front. Too,
it was hoped that large-scale amphibious operations behind an
advancing Soviet-led army might stall the attack, or even force a
withdrawal. Clearly such operations would have been quite risky. To
make them viable, the Maritime Strategy envisaged the destruction of
Soviet naval forces as early as possible in a war; after that NATO
could have afforded the significant naval losses associated with flanking
attacks. There was a historical precedent. Several times during World
War I the Royal Navy contemplated a flanking amphibious operation.
In each case it had to abandon such plans as too dangerous, because
the likely loss of ships would have caused a loss of superiority over
the German fleet, which in turn would have created a disastrous
situation (the German surface fleet would, for example, have been
even more effective in commerce-raiding than were the U-boats).
Conversely, had the Royal Navy succeeded in destroying the German
High Seas Fleet at, say, Jutland, it could then have supported a flanking
operation, which might have broken the stalemate on the Western
Front in, say, 1917. Unfortunately, this possibility was not well
appreciated after the end of World War I; it seemed to too many that
the Royal Navy had played a passive role while the British Army

suffered in France. Too, the Royal Navy was unable to explain the vital role of its battle fleet as the covering force for the convoy escorts which broke the U-boat offensive. Without that covering force, the escorts (weak because they had to be numerous) could not have survived any blow by the German surface fleet. This, too, was not a theoretical point. In World War II the US Navy conducted an extremely successful submarine offensive against Japan, despite the loss of eighteen months of effort to defective torpedoes. The Japanese were never able to provide adequate convoy escorts, largely because ships were so desperately needed to deal with the assaults of the US main fleet. Although those assaults did not sink many merchant ships, they performed a vital synergistic function. Had the Japanese succeeded in neutralizing the attacking US fleet, they would probably also have been able to solve their submarine problem.

3   This may seem to reverse the point about invisibility above. That is not the case. Ships become invisible, in effect, when they pass beyond the horizon: visibility is generally voluntary. However, the emphasis on presence may be an argument against extensive investment in stealth. That is, ships on presence missions are generally not at war; they must show themselves to be effective. The other side decides when to go to war, when to fire at the ship on station. Unless the ship can suddenly become invisible as the missile approaches, stealth may have little relevance in such a situation (so, too, may active defence, since it may be inappropriate to fire until it is far too late; passive protection would seem to be vital).

4   These tasks require a combination of wide-area surveillance and ships to act as interceptors. The former is similar in principle to the surveillance of the Soviet fleet carried on by NATO during the Cold War, and it employs many of the same techniques. Mechanisms include sea-surveillance satellites and maritime patrol aircraft, feeding data into intelligence fusion centres ashore, which in turn provide their picture of sea traffic to deployed warships. Because much of the data is inevitably somewhat time-late, the recipients have to modify it to merge it properly into their own tactical pictures, on the basis of which they act. Newly important tasks such as drug interdiction involve much the same requirements and resources. The Gulf War embargo was probably the first to exploit work done mainly by the US Navy in developing sea surveillance on the basis described here; the shipboard end of the system was the Joint Operational Tactical System (JOTS), which received a high-level intelligence broadcast. JOTS was deployed remarkably quickly specifically to support the embargo; that in turn was possible because it was largely software running on a standard US computer, which already existed in quantity (software is easy to reproduce).

5   SPY-l is unique among US Navy search radars in that its data is sufficient for fire control. This degree of precision inspired the development of

CEC, which was originally intended to allow a fleet in the Norwegian Sea to make maximum use of the missiles on board. The problem was that it would probably be impossible to transfer missiles from ship to ship in anything approximating rough weather, so there had to be a fear that individual ships would exhaust their missile supplies before the battle or campaign ended. CEC also inspired the concept of the arsenal ship, in effect an ammunition ship to reinforce the fleet without having to risk the physical transfer of its missiles to the firing ships (with CEC, they could fire its weapons remotely). The limit to Aegis systems was later lifted; a CEC net, for example, can include airborne early warning aircraft (E-2Cs) and also ships limited to point-defence missiles, such as carriers.

6   Littoral anti-submarine warfare is further complicated because the likeliest targets, diesel submarines, provide far less distinctive signatures than nuclear units. Navies are placing renewed emphasis on active sonar, and there is fresh interest in techniques by means of which an active sonar can automatically identify a target, particularly a bottomed target, as a submarine. Multi-statics may offer some hope of imaging.

7   Shells are to be GPS-guided. One hope of holding down cost is to use inertial devices (accelerometers and gyros) derived from those used in anti-lock automobile brakes. Range is needed not only to deal with targets well back from the coast but also to keep the valuable surface combatants over the horizon, well clear of shore-based anti-ship missiles. This latter requirement led the US Navy to develop and deploy air-cushion landing craft and, later, to develop a fast amphibian vehicle, the AAAV. In turn, the capacity to attack from beyond the horizon allows an amphibious group offshore to threaten a wide swath of coast (and the air-cushion vehicle can climb a wider variety of beaches than in the past). Both considerations may complicate defence to the point that an enemy cannot decide where to lay mines and where to deploy defending forces. In that case more of the defender's burden will fall on his own mobile forces, such as tactical aircraft and theatre ballistic missiles.

8   Ships are tending towards an open architecture which can be upgraded without recourse to an expensive modernisation. It thus becomes reasonable to build ships for long operating lives, in the expectation that they can be kept up to date by piecemeal, gradual, improvement in their sensors, command systems, and weapons. That would seem particularly important in an era in which a navy must cover numerous nearly simultaneous crises but cannot expect to receive many new ships each year. For example, if ships last 20 years, a navy must receive two new ships each year to maintain a fleet of 40. If they last 40 years, the annual figure is halved. Long life, of course, is not easy to achieve, since the ship must be designed so that she is easy to update. Vertical launchers are a step in that direction. So is the substitution of data busses (combat system highways in the RN) for the earlier point-

-to-point wiring: it is far easier to plug a new device into a bus than to rewire a ship. The adoption of distributed multi-computer combat direction systems, as in the SSCS in a Type 23 frigate, is also a step in this direction, since such systems are easier to modify and upgrade than are the central computer systems of the past. A ship intended for long life and open architecture is likely to be larger than earlier ones, but on the other hand it should prove a much better bargain over its lifetime; it is also likely to be more survivable in combat (partly because it has been built to survive longer service). The situation is simplified by the fact that ship steel is quite cheap; larger ships cost more only because their sheer size tempts navies to stuff more into them. Now unit costs may fall for two reasons. First, open-architecture vertical launchers may not have to be filled completely in peacetime. Second, electronic hardware is becoming much less expensive; the highest cost is now borne by software. However, software costs essentially nothing to reproduce. In a distributed system, modification is incremental and may be relatively inexpensive. It therefore pays to buy as many identical ships as possible, spreading the cost of software over the largest possible class.

9   It is only fair to point out that several revolutionary hull developments of the past, which seemed likely to dominate future construction, have never fulfilled their early promise. Examples include big hydrofoils (for frigates) and surface effect ships. Both are still classed as advanced hull forms, and both retain some advocates.

The Influence of Law on Maritime Operations

Steven Haines

Most human activity today is regulated with a far higher degree of intensity than ever before. Law is proliferating rapidly and that dealing with the regulation of maritime activity is no exception. Those charged with the conduct of naval operations are not exempt from this process. Indeed, a sizeable proportion of the operations being conducted today have arisen as a direct consequence of legal developments since the end of the Second World War. There has been a gradual, at times exponential, increase in the amount of public international law dealing with maritime activity. The 1970s were especially busy times for those involved with negotiating new law and a great deal of interest was generated about how it would influence the way navies would go about their business.

In 1974, when the Third UN Conference on the Law of the Sea (UNCLOS III) was only just getting underway,[1] the then Chichele Professor of International Law at Oxford, D P O'Connell. himself a former naval officer, called for:

> "a continuing dialogue between lawyers who know enough of what goes on in the operations room of a warship and naval officers who have sufficient awareness of the advantages and inhibitions of the law, to bring the necessary professional insight into the influence of law on sea power."[2]

Few appreciated better than O'Connell the relationship between law and seapower. Sadly, he died in 1979 before the full consequences of UNCLOS III had been revealed. Nevertheless, the essential features of the *1982 UN Convention on the Law of the Sea* were already in place by then and it was obvious that naval officers would in future have to take an even greater interest in legal factors when conducting operations at and from the sea.

However, despite the substantial changes in the legal order of the oceans precipitated by UNCLOS III, the essential elements of international law having a bearing on the conduct of maritime operations still fall into the two pre-existing categories: the laws of war and neutrality at sea, and those parts of the law of peace that are relevant to the maritime environment. It is within the latter category that *1982 UNCLOS* falls; it had nothing to do with the laws of war,[3] despite having a profound influence on the conduct of maritime operations.

The traditional distinction between laws relating to war and those dealing with normal peacetime circumstances has its origins in the earliest texts of modern international law, in particular Hugo Grotius's *De Jure Belli ac Pacis*. That said, in recent years, especially since 1945, the clear distinction between the laws of war and the laws of peace has become blurred, despite an understandable reluctance to abandon it altogether.[4] The principal cause of the blurring of the distinction between war and peace has been the establishment of the United Nations, in particular the drafting of its Charter and the assumption within it that combat operations could only in future be legitimate if mounted in self defence or for the enforcement of UN endorsed sanctions. In the post-1945 UN legal order, theoretically war is outlawed. Arguably, therefore, there should not be any law governing its conduct.

Operation *Desert Storm*, for example, was a UN endorsed response to an illegal invasion of Kuwait. At sea there might have appeared to be rival belligerents; the conflict is commonly referred to as the 'Gulf War' and the Iraqi Navy certainly came under attack from coalition naval forces. Nevertheless, by strict interpretation of UN law, it was not a war and there could be no neutrals in the conflict.[5] With one or two minor or idiosyncratic exceptions, all states are members of the UN and, even those not involved in the coalition, were under a legal obligation, through UN Security Council resolutions, not to support Iraq. In the South Atlantic in 1982, in which only two states (Britain and Argentina) were locked in conflict, it is again arguable that the laws of neutrality did not apply. By the principles of international law established in 1945 no other state could claim neutrality in relation to the conflict; all should have recognised the UK as the injured party and the British operations as a legitimate response to Argentina's illegitimate refusal to comply with UN

Security Council resolutions. If it is not possible to be strictly neutral, the traditional distinction between neutrals and belligerents loses much of its meaning.

Nevertheless, legal theory aside, the practical distinctions between the laws of peace and the laws of war – and those between neutrals and belligerents – retain their relevance. It is clearly still possible for conflict to break out between states and for no UN action to be taken to legitimise the actions of one side or the other; a mere veto by a permanent Security Council member can effectively stall that process. Differing interpretations can be placed on claims to the right of self defence which can lead to two sides in a conflict both claiming to be exercising it. For that reason alone it makes sense for the laws of war and neutrality at sea to retain their validity. There is also the important distinction within the laws of war between *Jus ad Bello* and *Jus in Bellum*. The former deals with the legality of recourse to war and the latter (often referred to as international humanitarian law because of its concern, among other things, with the protection of vulnerable persons during conflict) covers the conduct of military operations once hostilities have broken out. *Jus in Bellum* retain their importance because, even under the UN Charter, the exercise of self defence and the conduct of Chapter VII sanctions operations may result in armed conflict short of war.

Additionally, in situations similar to the conflict in the South Atlantic in 1982, neither side would necessarily wish to involve innocent third party shipping. Regardless of the legal niceties, it would be politically risky for those involved in such a conflict simply to ignore the traditional principles of neutrality; they would find it difficult to either gain or retain international sympathy for their cause while interfering with or launching unprovoked attacks on uninvolved/ innocent third party shipping. In theory, while the laws of neutrality at sea should have become irrelevant, they are still regarded as necessary.

While the laws of war and neutrality at sea remain relevant, there is still an unquestionable blurring of the distinctions between peace and war/armed conflict and the laws relevant to each condition. For clarity of understanding, most navies in their guidance to operational commanders prefer to deal with the laws of war and the laws of peace separately, despite the existence of a grey area between the two conditions. The US Navy, for example, divides its manual of the law of naval operations into two distinct parts, the first dealing with the 'Law of Peacetime Naval Operations' and the second (still in preparation) dealing with the 'Law of Naval Warfare'.[6] The Royal Navy is currently revising its equivalent handbook following UK accession to *1982 UNCLOS* and it is more than likely that the distinction will again be retained.[7]

This makes practical sense in the quest for basic understanding of the rules of law. There is an obvious difference between rules that govern the normal peacetime conduct of navigation through territorial seas, international straits and archipelagic waters and other rules that deal with legal limitations on the use of force in conflict. But, where the two types of rule come into play together the distinction may not always be entirely clear. If, for example, a warship which is exercising a legitimate right of unimpeded transit passage through a strategically important international strait is prevented from proceeding by a warship belonging to the coastal state, what rights does it have to resist interference in order to effect transit? There is invariably a right of self defence. If the warship from the coastal state attempts to prevent transit by manoeuvring and harassing, but does not threaten to open fire, what action can the commanding officer of the transiting vessel take? Notwithstanding any strategic political ingredient in the decision to order the warship to transit the strait (to assert a right in response to a threat of deprivation, for example[8]) he has a legal obligation to limit his response to actions in proportion to the threat posed. It would, for example, probably be contrary to international law for him to open fire and sink the vessel harassing him. Ironically, if he did open fire, the commanding officer of the coastal state's warship may be perfectly entitled to exercise his own rights of self defence and open fire in return.

Such a situation is not inconceivable. The extension of territorial sea width to 12 nautical miles in *1982 UNCLOS* has had the effect of enclosing within territorial jurisdiction the waters of a number of strategically important international straits. Equally important has been the creation of archipelagic states and the establishment of rights of passage through waters enclosed within their baselines.[9]

The rights of straits transit passage and archipelagic transit passage exist in law and coastal/archipelagic states are under an obligation to permit it. But a coastal state's illegitimate attempt to prevent passage does not create a right for others to force passage using unlimited force. To use a hypothetical domestic legal example by way of illustration, a rambler attempting to use a legitimate right of way over a farmer's land would be committing murder if, in response to harassment from the farmer, his reaction was to shoot him dead. Incidents involving the assertion of transit rights combine considerations of the laws of peace (the law of the sea) with elements of the laws of war (the need to act proportionately when acting in self defence).

Interestingly, what has happened in the last twenty five years in particular, is that the law of the sea, developed to regulate maritime activity in conditions of peace, has created additional rights and obligations that have substantially enhanced the legal complexity of the maritime environment. This has certainly helped to regulate maritime activity for the general good. It has also greatly increased the range of tasks performed by navies. Effective maritime domain[10] management is achieved through regulation and enforcement. Coastal policing operations are frequently undertaken by navies; indeed, for many states they are the principal reason for acquiring and maintaining naval forces.[11] However, on occasions the enhanced legal complexity of the maritime environment may actually increase tension in circumstances where previously there would have been no potential for it to do so.

The law has not developed in a vacuum, of course. The Icelandic Government, for example, did not progressively extend its jurisdiction over coastal fisheries for the sheer hell of it; it did so in order to impose an effective fish stock management regime in the absence of any workable alternative. Those decisions provoked successive reactions by the UK Government and led to the so-called Cod Wars between the two states. Resource disputes could flare up in several regions around the world. Navies may become involved on both sides of those disputes as some states attempt to restrict rights and others attempt to exercise them by force.

Naval officers at sea acting tactically, commanders functioning at the operational level and higher level decision makers at the military strategic and grand strategic level, all need to recognise the possibility that peacetime operations might escalate into conflict. The line between what one might refer to as 'peaceful tension' and armed conflict might be crossed without either side considering the academic distinction between them. There may be no time for such deliberations. Post-*de facto* analysis may pinpoint a decisive moment of transition to conflict but that is of no use to those involved at the time. In effect, there is no line to be crossed. There is instead a process of escalating tension that forms a spectrum ranging from entirely peaceful activity at one end to outright armed combat at the other. The law is superimposed upon this spectrum. It can be used to limit the extent or rate at which escalation occurs. It must also be applied appropriately at whatever point along that spectrum the opposing forces find themselves. Looked at from a legal perspective, there is close relationship, just short of symbiosis, between the level of tension at any given moment and the influence of the law on that situation.

Increasingly, since the end of the Cold War, the maritime strategic emphasis has shifted from open ocean and deep water maritime operations towards operations closer to coastal regions. In the US and in the UK in particular, established Cold War concerns with the threat posed by Soviet naval forces in the North Atlantic have been replaced by a concentration of effort on so-called littoral operations.[12] Bearing in mind previous extensions of coastal state jurisdiction and influence over those very waters in which littoral operations will be conducted, the legal issues that will need to be borne in mind by commanders at all levels will involve not just those to do with combat operations but a great many additional considerations to do with rights and correlative obligations of coastal states as well. Both the increase in the amount and complexity of law impinging on maritime operations, and the shift towards operations within other states' maritime domains, present maritime commanders with additional legal burdens. Maritime operations are conducted in an environment that is profoundly affected by the law. As O'Connell noted over twenty years ago:

> "Naval staffs must....be equipped to handle the legal aspects of naval planning, whether it be in the matter of drafting rules of engagement or in their interpretation. The machinery must be

devised for rapid appreciation of the legal issues and equally rapid reaction if the theory of self defence is to be effectively translated into terms of sea power. Above all, reflection must develop concerning the ways in which technology influences the modes of self defence and the ways in which the intensifying ambiguities of the law of the sea influence decisions....."[13]

While it is, of course, necessary for both lawyers and naval officers to understand the, at times, subtle relationships between law and force at sea, it is also an area in which higher level decision makers need to be competent – and that includes those advising political policy makers. The effective management of crisis situations, especially those that are moving towards the transition from 'peaceful tension' to armed conflict, is profoundly important.

In recent years the translation of strategic desires into action at the tactical level has been achieved through mechanisms known as Rules of Engagement (ROE). The term 'ROE' is a relatively recent addition to the military glossary. Naval officers at sea have for centuries acted under instructions from their political masters and their superior commanders; conceptually, there is nothing new about ROE. However, the modern form of ROE, and the term itself, have their origins in the 1960s, with the UK at the forefront of their development.[14] They are certainly now a constant feature of maritime operations involving NATO navies with, for example, all RN units at sea acting in accordance with either standard peacetime ROE or with specific ROE promulgated for use in particular operations. The same can also be said of other, non-NATO, maritime coalition operations, especially those involving some level of involvement by NATO member states. The US Navy's Doctrine Command has been developing NATO's EXTAC 1000 Series for use by the majority of the world's navies when operating in multinational maritime forces. It is the intention that an additional publication in this series will deal with the subject of ROE, something with which several navies remain less than entirely familiar.[15] The Russian Navy, as well as using the doctrine and procedures worked up by NATO and the USN Doctrine Command, will also be discussing the development of ROE in the context of the Anglo-Russian Naval Initiative announced in November 1997. Clearly, the ROE process, while far from universally adopted, is becoming increasingly familiar ground for navies worldwide.

ROE are not exclusively about the application of legal rules in operational circumstances, but legal considerations most certainly represent a vital ingredient in the mix of factors that go into their drafting. With modern technology permitting the rapid communication of changes to ROE, it is possible for strategic decision makers to initiate tactical action. Equally, it is possible for tactical decisions to have immediate strategic effect. The speed at which such decisions and their effects can be communicated has generated a need for a sure and competent understanding of the legal restraints on action and the potential for leverage that the appropriate use of the law represents.

O'Connell recognised its potential to both restrict and enhance naval utility over twenty years ago. Nothing has diminished its impact since then. Indeed, if anything, the influence of law on contemporary maritime operations is even more profound today than it was in the past.

1   It was not until twenty years later that the *1982 UN Convention on the Law of the Sea* entered into force, in 1994. The UK did not acceded until 1997.

2   D P O'Connell, *The Influence of Law on Seapower*, Manchester University Press, 1975, p. 189.

3   Indeed, the Conference deliberately kept off the subject. After UNCLOS III (between 1988–94), the International Institute of Humanitarian Law attempted to update the laws of war at sea through the convening of a team of international lawyers and naval experts. The results have been published as: L Doswald-Beck (Ed), *The San Remo Manual on International Law Applicable to Armed Conflicts at Sea*, Grotius Publications/Cambridge University Press, 1995. While not having the status of an international convention, the manual is having a significant influence on the content of individual states' manuals on the laws of war at sea and should be regarded as an essential source of opinion on the current state of the law in this area.

4   The latest edition of *Openheim's International Law*, for example, is still retaining an element of that distinction, with the 9th Edition of Vol. 1, published in 1992, covering the Law of Peace, although the intended 8th Edition of Vol. 2 will admittedly deal with "disputes and armed conflict" rather than with the 'Law of War'. (Sir R Jennings and Sir A Watts (Eds), *Oppenheim's International Law: Vol. 1 Peace (Introduction and Part 1)*, 9th Edition, Longman, London, 1992, p.xiii.)

5   See N Ronzitti, "The Crisis of the Traditional Law Regulating International Armed Conflicts at Sea and the Need for its Revision" in N Ronzitti (Ed), *The Law of Naval Warfare: A Collection of Agreements and Documents with Commentaries*, Martinus Nijhoff, Dordrecht, 1988, p. 6.

6   *The Commander's Handbook on the Law of Naval Operations*, Department of the Navy (NWP 1–14M), October 1995. The handbook was published simultaneously by the US Marine Corps and the US Department of Transport (US Coast Guard) under the same title but with different alpha-numeric codes: FMFM 1–10 and COMDTPUB P5800.7 respectively.

7   *BR3012: Guide to Maritime Law*. This author is coordinating the production of a new edition of this manual. It will incorporate a section on the Laws of War at Sea based on the relevant Maritime Warfare chapters of the UK's new *Manual of the Law of Armed Conflict* (Chapters 13–17 in the latest draft of the Manual, which has yet to be published).

8   Naval forces have certainly been used in the past to assert rights of

transit through waters claimed by other states. The Corfu Channel Incident is one example; so too are US 6th Fleet deployments into the Gulf of Sirte as challenges to Libyan claims to sovereignty. All the major maritime powers are likely to object to coastal states enhancing their control of adjacent waters and may choose to demonstrate resolve by deliberately sailing warships through waters to assert their rights to do so.

9   Important examples of strategically important archipelagic states are Indonesia and the Philippines. Without secured passage rights through the waters within these archipelagic states, strategic mobility would be severely hampered affecting both merchant shipping and navies. Transit distances from the Western Pacific into the Indian Ocean would be increased substantially if these archipelagic waters, together with the Singapore and Malacca Straits, were closed for transit. See: J H Noer and D Gregory, *Chokepoints: Maritime Economic concerns in Southeast Asia*, National Defense University Press, Washington DC, 1996.

10   The 'maritime domain' consists of those zones of coastal jurisdiction claimed by a coastal state. The term was coined originally by this author in his doctoral thesis (*Military Aid to Civil Authorities in Britain's Maritime Domain*, University of Aberdeen, 1992) a brief summary of which was published as: S W Haines, "Exercising Coastal State Jurisdiction: The Use of the Military in Britain's Maritime Domain", *GeoJournal*, Vol. 37, No. 2, (October 1995), pp. 247–255.

11   In this context the term 'naval forces' should be regarded as including any maritime forces that are involved in maritime domain management, including those officially a part of a state's coastguard and other 'non-naval' institutions.

12   Strictly speaking the 'littoral' is "of or on the shore"; "the region lying along the shore" (*Oxford English Dictionary*). However, the term has in recent years developed a broader meaning in the military strategic context. One current definition is "The area from the open ocean which must be controlled to support operations ashore, and the area inland from shore that can be defended and supported directly from the sea" (*BR1806: The Fundamentals of British Maritime Doctrine, HMSO*, London, 1995, p. 221). In this military strategic sense the littoral is a flexible concept, the geographical extent of which will depend very much on the particular circumstances to which the term is applied. In one sense the 'littoral region' can be described as a product of a coastal operational state of mind: one instinctively knows when one is in it because of the range and nature of operational challenges and opportunities one has to confront.

13   D P O'Connell, as Note 2.

14   Interestingly, the UK Naval Staff history of the Cod Wars between the UK and Iceland makes the point that in 1958 the term ROE was not used (although instructions were issued to naval commanders deployed in Icelandic waters). By the early 1970s, and the final round of 'cod wars', the term had entered into currency and ROE's "incorporation in......the orders was a matter of routine." (*BR1736(57) Naval Staff History: The Cod War – Naval Operations in Support of the British Fishing Industry (1958–76)*, Directorate of Naval Staff Duties (D/NHB/11/6/13) UK Ministry of Defence, London, 1990, p. 172.)

15   The 1000 Series EXTACS (or Experimental Tactics) publications were originally developed for use by those non-NATO states involved in Partnership for Peace operations. All the documents previously designated as NATO 1000 Series EXTACS have now been redesignated as 'Multinational Maritime Manuals' (MMMs), are all free of a security classification and have been made available to any navy that wishes to use them. The international staff at USN Doctrine Command have also worked up a 'capping publication' (*Multinational Maritime Operations Manual* (MMOPs), US Department of the Navy, Naval Doctrine Command, Norfolk, September 1996) which has been made available on the Doctrine Command's Internet site: http://www.ndc.navy.mil. The additional document on international law and ROE is currently in early draft form and is entitled *Use of Force and Multinational Maritime Operations*.

Naval Aviation

Tim Benbow

Air power made its major wartime debut in the First World War. Its initial performance at sea was faltering and far from decisive but suggested great promise for the future. Aircraft, both heavier and lighter than air, assisted the battlefleet by scouting for the enemy and spotting for gunfire. They also patrolled against U-boats and, more effectively, escorted convoys once these were formed. Some attacks were made on targets ashore, with increasing effect. By the end of the war the Royal Navy had come to attach considerable importance to aviation, and the Grand Fleet deployed large numbers of aeroplanes on capital ships, cruisers and the first aircraft carriers.

Although the interwar period saw bitter arguments about the effect of air power on navies, the Second World War removed any doubt that aircraft, with their advantages of mobility, speed and elevation, had fundamentally changed naval power and had also become a vital part of it. Some of the roles which naval aviation now undertook were developments from those first attempted in the previous war. Others represented a new departure and restored to navies some of the ground lost as a result of industrialisation in the second half of the nineteenth century, which had elevated Land Power and continental powers at the expense of Sea Power and maritime powers.

First, in World War II naval aviation provided an increasingly effective solution to certain long-standing problems of the battle fleet in defeating its enemy counterpart. It allowed the enemy to be located, tracked, brought to battle, and then, with his line disrupted by air attack, sunk either by gunfire or by aircraft themselves, which increasingly became the principal strike weapon of the fleet. Moreover, aircraft proved able to sink warships in port, where an inferior fleet had hitherto been able to seek refuge. Second, naval aviation provided a counter to some serious technological threats to surface ships. Aircraft operating from shore bases or escort carriers, particularly when they were equipped with radar, were central in the defeat of the U-boats around the North Atlantic convoys. A newer menace in this war was land-based air power: ships operating within range of land-based aircraft were frequently subject to attack by bombs, torpedoes and mines, or by surface warships and submarines alerted by aerial reconnaissance. This danger often imposed significant constraints on the operation of warships and merchant shipping alike. Aircraft were a major part of the response to this threat too, either in the form of land-based fighter cover or, in the many areas which were out of range of friendly air bases, carrier-borne fighters. Thus, aircraft played a large part in the defence against air attack at sea just as they did on land.

Naval aviation therefore became central to the struggle to control sea communications, helping to locate and destroy hostile fleets, surface raiders, submarines and aircraft. Yet perhaps a more dramatic development was in power projection, with naval aviation providing a devastating new means of bombarding coastal and inland targets, including air and naval bases. The mobility of aircraft carriers and their ability to concentrate formidable air power re-established the viability of amphibious operations as a major element of warfare, which had been widely questioned in the aftermath of the First World War. Hence, by the end of the war the battleship had been supplanted by the aircraft carrier as the heart of the fleet. Even though the older capital ship still had important uses, carriers could better perform its fundamental task of fighting the enemy fleet and in addition proved they could both counter threats to the use of the sea (particularly submarines and air attack) and elevate power projection to a new level of effectiveness.

The United States ended the war with by far the strongest fleet, centred on the large carriers that had fought with such conspicuous success in the Pacific. Throughout the Cold War the carrier battle groups of the US Navy held an important place in peacetime deterrence and in war plans, both in securing command of the seas and in projecting force in support of NATO flanks or against targets inside the USSR. The US Navy was strongly orientated to power projection, with even its planned contribution to defending sea communications mainly taking the form of attacks upon Soviet air and submarine forces at their source.[1]   There was some scepticism both about the ability of carriers to survive in the face of the threats they would face and about the contribution that they could make to a land war in Europe. Nonetheless, it is clear that the Soviet Union took the threat posed by US naval aviation immensely seriously and devoted enormous resources to countering it, which was one of the main reasons for the expansion of the Soviet Navy. The US Navy also saw widespread service outside Europe, in major and lesser regional conflicts and in forward presence in support of American diplomacy. The geography of the United States and her global web of alliances and interests ensured that maritime power, with naval aviation at its core, tended to be the force of choice for intervention.[2]

In 1945 Britain was acknowledged to be one of the "Big Three" military powers but the emerging post-war picture was far less favourable. Immediate problems of demobilisation were exacerbated by growing economic difficulties which made sustaining the cost of world-wide commitments increasingly onerous. Moreover, a series of technological developments, not least in carrier-borne aircraft, had to be evaluated and incorporated, which placed yet more strain on a national budget in which defence was becoming less of a priority. At the same time, a new continental threat emerged in the form of the USSR, which once again Britain could only meet by concentrating efforts in Europe at the expense of more distant interests. Yet in spite of all this, the Royal Navy has remained either second or (when the Soviet fleet displaced the UK from that spot) third in the world. Given the plethora of economic, political and military problems that Britain faced, it is perhaps remarkable that her naval power did not decline to a greater extent than it did.[3]

Clearly Britain was operating on a different scale to that of the United States in naval power as in other military spheres. In addition, there were significant differences of emphasis in the roles of the two navies. Nevertheless, some parallels may be found between the British experience since 1945 and that of the United States. For both countries, the central planning concern was war with the USSR. Whereas the US Navy tended in this context to focus more on support of the land battle, the Royal Navy placed primary emphasis on the defence of sea communications in the approaches to the UK and, in the early years of the Cold War, the Mediterranean. Carrier aviation was central to this effort, particularly for the air defence of convoys and anti-submarine warfare outside the limited radius of land-based aircraft. The British carriers also operated strike aircraft, though their envisaged role was mainly against enemy surface units and naval and air bases, with support of NATO forces ashore a secondary concern.

Direct war against the USSR, however, was only one aspect of the Royal Navy's responsibilities. British defence policy aimed to deter or, failing that, to be ready to fight a "Hot War" but principally sought to promote wider foreign policy objectives and to fight the Cold War, particularly in the Near and Far East. The government's analysis of the threat was that direct Communist attack was less probable than attempts to weaken the Western powers around the peripheries, and these had to be countered.[4] Britain could meet some such challenges on its own, as in Malaya, but in larger wars it could only support the United States. So, like its larger ally, the Royal Navy with its air power saw frequent use around the world.

In Korea, the Royal Navy took on a role remarkably similar to that which it had performed in the Pacific War (and would again in the 1991 Gulf War) – a significant and politically desirable, though not militarily indispensable, auxiliary to the US Navy. British Commonwealth naval aviation performed a remarkably effective role, with a proportionately higher sortie rate than the much larger American force.[5] This war showed that there could be a need to fight outside Europe and that carriers could operate air power where land-based aircraft could not reach, giving them immense value for Britain as for the United States. Subsequent British plans stressed heavy carriers:

> whose great mobility and offensive power, to be augmented by guided missiles and by the other modern equipment which is under development, will add powerfully to our ability to hit the enemy either independently or in support of allied land forces and land-based air forces.

This applied particularly to limited wars such as Korea, where the Navy, "can provide, by reason of its mobility, powerful assistance to the land battle."[6]

A few years after the end of the Korean War, Britain was again engaged in a regional conflict with a significant maritime component, though this time as the senior coalition partner. The Suez operation of 1956 involved five British and French carriers with 18 squadrons of aircraft, in addition to 38 squadrons deployed to Malta and Cyprus. Two further British carriers, converted to operate as commando carriers, pioneered the technique of helicopter-borne assault. Once again, the Royal Navy's power projection capability proved its value, particularly carrier aviation, which showed "the versatility of sea/air power, demonstrating the advantages of the mobile carrier force", as naval aircraft flew 2,000 sorties.[7]

The value of carriers was recognised even by Defence Secretary Duncan Sandys. In view of his previous hostility towards naval aviation, it is striking that in 1957 he came to accept that without the Fleet Air Arm, "the Navy would be converted from a fighting fleet into a maritime police force".[8] Although the 1957 White Paper held the role of the navy in total war to be "somewhat uncertain", it acknowledged that either before a nuclear exchange or after an indecisive one there would be a need to defend Atlantic communications against submarine attack. Yet the carrier force was justified primarily by reference to Britain's global commitments:

> On account of its mobility, the Royal Navy, together with the Royal Marines, provides another effective means of bringing power rapidly to bear in peacetime emergencies or limited hostilities. In modern conditions the role of the aircraft carrier, which is in effect a mobile air station, becomes increasingly significant.[9]

Limited war east of Suez therefore became the principal rationale for the Royal Navy's carriers. However, these vessels needed aircraft capable of defeating their likely opposition, which increasingly meant jet aircraft. These were larger and heavier than those for which wartime carriers had been designed; several existing carriers would not be able to operate modern jet aircraft even after extensive modernisation.[10] The current force of carriers could get by for a few more years , and hence the legacy of the wartime fleet would continue to mask the dilemmas of British defence policy for a little longer. However, the new ships and aircraft would be very expensive at a time of increasingly intense competition within the defence budget. The RAF, on the verge of losing its responsibility for the nuclear deterrent, was also looking for a role in limited war east of Suez. Nevertheless, after intense inter-Service argument, in 1963 the RAF's "island base scheme" was rejected and a new carrier was announced – CVA-01, which would displace 53,000 tons and carry about 40 aircraft.[11]

Naval aviation therefore played a leading role for Britain in both plans for global war and regional intervention but financial realities began to call the latter into question: intervention on the scale of Suez was moving beyond Britain's plausible aspirations. The problems came to a head with a new government which sought to reduce expenditure and which reversed the 1963 conclusion, deciding that land-based aircraft offered a cheaper and more effective alternative to naval aviation. The 1966 Defence White Paper forswore the option of major power projection operations without allies, the only type of operation for which it held carriers to be essential. It announced that although the current carriers would continue in service, they would not be replaced at the end of their lifetimes, and CVA-01 was cancelled. The depleted navy would rely on missiles against surface ships; helicopters operating from destroyers and cruisers would carry out anti-submarine tasks; and the other roles of carrier aviation – air defence, early warning, reconnaissance and strike – would be performed by land-based F-111 aircraft.[12]

This decision rested on two related misconceptions. First, although it was true that Britain could no longer realistically aspire to a major independent power projection capability, it was not the case that these were the only operations for which carriers were needed. Ironically, even the 1966 White Paper recognised this. *Part I: The Defence Review* stated that there was only one type of operation for which carriers were indispensable: "the landing, or withdrawal, of troops against sophisticated opposition outside the range of land-based air cover", and Britain could not undertake such operations even if she could afford a larger carrier force.[13] However, *Part II: The Defence Estimates* noted that:

The carrier is the most important element of the Fleet *for offensive action against an enemy at sea or ashore, and makes a large contribution to the defence of our seaborne forces.* It can also play an important part in operations where local air superiority has to be gained and maintained and offensive support of ground forces is required.[14]

As explained above, the Royal Navy's use since 1945 had been in limited operations or as part of a multinational force, as it had been in Korea and Suez (and, indeed, in the Second World War after 1941). The Review underestimated the role of carrier aviation in supporting these tasks of sea power which remained important even if Britain was no longer to undertake major independent military interventions.

Second, it was incorrect to claim that land-based aircraft could satisfactorily perform all the maritime roles of carrier aviation. The second Defence Statement of 1967 argued:

> Air power will be as indispensable to the Fleet of tomorrow as it is today. [...] After the last carriers go, the Royal Navy, like the Army, will rely on Royal Air Force land-based aircraft to support it.[15]

This rests on an erroneous comparison: the navy is not like the army, and requires a different kind of air support. Land-based aircraft can perform some of the tasks of organic naval aviation, and may achieve even more as a complement to it, but cannot adequately perform all its roles. Aircraft operating from shore bases have shortcomings which could easily become grave, such as their basic dependence on unrestricted access to secure bases in the theatre, and their less certain availability and inferior responsiveness compared to organic aircraft. The F-111 force may have been cheaper than carrier aircraft but this reduced expenditure did not offer the same capabilities.

In any case, this debate was rendered moot by Britain's deepening financial crisis. In 1967 the government announced the phasing out of the east of Suez commitments, and in February 1968 decided to hasten this planned withdrawal and to cut defence spending further, with the carriers to be paid off by 1972 and the F-111 order cancelled.[16]

Nevertheless, organic naval aviation survived in the British fleet. The same review that announced the demise of aircraft carriers in the navy which had pioneered them, recognised that some form of organic aviation would be needed for operations in the face of the more sophisticated threats that were emerging. A new cruiser (as it was initially termed) was designed to operate an anti-submarine helicopter which would be too large for destroyers or frigates, and also to provide command and control capabilities and a platform for the new *Sea Dart* air-defence missile.[17] By the early 1970s it was being stated that these ships would also be able to operate the *Harrier* vertical take-off aircraft, which would "add considerably to the interception, reconnaissance, probe and strike capability of the Fleet at sea", for example, allowing a task force to shoot down shadowing Soviet reconnaissance aircraft.[18] The primary role of the cruisers was described as "command ship of ASW forces", but their missiles and aircraft would also "enable them to contribute to area air defence and anti-surface ship operations".[19] Later, their flight decks were fitted with a "ski-jump" to allow the *Sea Harrier* to take off conventionally rather than vertically, thus increasing its load of weapons and fuel (hence it is more accurately termed STOVL, for Short Take Off, Vertical Landing). Older carriers which had been converted to the amphibious role were reconfigured to act as interim STOVL carriers until the new *Invincible* class appeared.

With the transition from the conventional aircraft carrier (the last of which, HMS *Ark Royal*, was paid off in 1978) to the STOVL/ helicopter carrier, the Royal Navy's aviation ceased to resemble a smaller version of the US carriers (like the French Navy and in the late 1980s, the final generation of Soviet carriers). Instead, it took up an alternative model which was also followed by the USSR (with their second-generation *Kiev* class carriers), the US Marine Corps, India, Spain, Italy and Thailand. These carriers allowed the Royal Navy to retain fixed-wing aviation, which was necessary for its intended operations in the potentially high-threat areas of the eastern Atlantic. By the late 1970s, the Royal Navy concentrated on anti-submarine warfare there, with its residual out of area capability a secondary justification.

Once again, however, doubts arose in some quarters about the value of naval aviation. The Thatcher government faced the familiar dilemma of trying to sustain extensive responsibilities with declining expenditure, at a time when the sophistication of the threat was steadily advancing. It acknowledged Britain's global interests but insisted that the priority had to remain Europe where the growing Soviet capability and the increasing complexity and cost of equipment were exacerbating Britain's position.[20] The gathering storm broke with the 1981 Nott defence review. Once again the nuclear deterrent and British forces in Germany were politically sacrosanct, so the navy came under renewed scrutiny. The government concluded that modern weapons posed an increasingly serious threat to warships and that many of the roles hitherto performed by surface vessels could be assigned to nuclear submarines and land-based aviation. Thus, the number of maritime aircraft and nuclear submarines would increase but the surface fleet would be drastically reduced: the carrier force would be cut, both assault ships would go (a decision which was soon reversed) and the number of escorts would shrink by a third.[21] The then US Secretary of the Navy exaggerated when he wrote that this would have left the Royal Navy a mere Coast Guard,[22] but it did represent a major loss of capability. Although two carriers were to be maintained, the underlying rationale of the review suggested that the long-term future of naval aviation could be seriously in doubt.

Yet again, events soon provided a compelling reminder that naval aviation fulfils certain operational requirements which other forces cannot wholly meet. In 1982, the Royal Navy was sent to the South Atlantic to fight precisely the war that it had been told would never again be necessary: the government required it to gain control of the sea and air surrounding the Falkland Islands and then to project power ashore, 9,000 miles from the UK and 5,000 miles outside the NATO area, but only 300 miles from the air and naval forces of a significant regional military power.

The aviation of the Falklands task force consisted primarily of two aircraft carriers (the last of the *Hermes* and the first of the *Invincible* class) with *Sea Harriers* and helicopters; other helicopters were carried in the escort, amphibious and supply ships. There was some limited support from land-based aircraft for maritime patrol, supply drops and a couple of strike missions, but the fact that the nearest available airfield was a 7,500 mile round trip away at Ascension

Island severely limited their contribution.[23]   The small force of *Sea Harriers* and the anti-aircraft missiles of the escorts, designed to operate under a much thicker umbrella of air cover, contained Argentine air power sufficiently effectively for an amphibious landing and ground campaign to retake the islands, although several escorts and supply ships were sunk or damaged.   The *Sea Harrier* performed a wide range of roles going far beyond that for which it had originally been designed.   It was used for fleet air defence, interception of aircraft challenging the blockade, reconnaissance over sea and land, attack on shipping, and strikes against land targets (in which role it was later supplemented by RAF *Harrier* GR3s).   Helicopters were used for many tasks, including anti-submarine warfare, attacks on ships, reconnaissance, special forces landing and support, amphibious assault, logistics and troop transportation, search and rescue, and missile countermeasures.

   The Falklands War showed that a force of surface ships carrying their own air power can operate successfully within range of significant land-based air opposition.   It reiterated one lesson of the Second World War: that attainment of the highest degree of sea control demands air supremacy and that in the absence of command of the air, maritime operations remain possible but are considerably more dangerous.   Yet even without complete control of the skies, the task force was able to carry out an amphibious landing and to prosecute a successful land campaign; the losses it suffered did not prevent the completion of its mission.   One of the principal conclusions to be drawn from the Falklands War is that organic naval aviation is essential for maritime operations that may face sophisticated opposition beyond the range of friendly air cover.   Given the advanced weapons that a modern fleet might have to face, some naval tasks, such as airborne early warning and air defence, must be carried out by aircraft which offer constant availability and a very high speed of response.   Land-based aircraft cannot always provide this.   Although suited to the eastern Atlantic because of the general availability of well-equipped air bases, even there they could not completely substitute for ship-borne aviation.   The latter also provides a more flexible asset, especially for out of area operations, in which (as the Falklands War demonstrated) the existence and availability of host nation support cannot be taken for granted.   The official report on the lessons of the war recognised that the gravest air defence problem had been the lack of airborne early warning aircraft, and announced the provision of helicopter-borne early warning radar for the carriers, the planned number of which was increased to three.[24]

For the UK between 1945 and 1990 there was an increasing tension between maintaining the continental commitment and supporting overseas interests. The primacy of the former led to a concentration within the defence budget on the forces perceived as most relevant for deterring global war – nuclear weapons, land-based aircraft and large, static ground forces. The main "hot war" preoccupation of the Royal Navy was the protection of NATO sea communications in the Atlantic (mainly against submarine attack) which was the most important justification for the carriers; their role in power projection, though useful, was secondary. In the late 1950s, however, any war was expected to be nuclear and the main rationale for the carriers became Britain's role east of Suez; when this was given up, the future of British naval aviation was thrown into doubt. Whilst the carriers that emerged from the upheavals of the 1960s were mainly intended for sea control, the 1981 review was based on the premise that this could be secured by other forces, particularly land-based aircraft. In the context of that time the review was probably correct to put a priority on Europe but it was mistaken in concluding that the only role for the carriers was out of area. There was a risk of underestimating the extent to which the continental forces depended on sea power, and the demise of the carriers would have jeopardised the Royal Navy's ability to contribute to a third Battle of the Atlantic. As it happened, the future of a three-carrier force and the survival of the surface fleet generally were assured by a war fought far from the east Atlantic. Yet even in local waters naval aviation offered various important capabilities that land-based aircraft could not duplicate.

British defence policy is no longer torn between Europe and interests further afield. British support for NATO continues but the end of the Soviet threat means that the forces required for this commitment are not continental ground and air forces which would fight where they are stationed, but rather more mobile and flexible forces which might need to fight anywhere in Europe or – more probably – beyond. Moreover, the spectrum of tasks which they have so far undertaken since the end of the Cold War, and which they will continue to face, has ranged from major regional conflict in the Gulf, through peace support operations in Bosnia, to crisis response with the reinforcement of Kuwait in the face of renewed Iraqi threats. The attributes this demands are the traditional comparative advantages of naval forces: mobility, reach, versatility, sustained presence, and independence of host nation support which might not be available.

Naval power is therefore particularly well suited to the demands of post-Cold War intervention. Perhaps the most important asset of navies is their ability to carry air power anywhere in the world, in international waters, on a self-contained air base, which reaches the theatre immediately ready for operations or, equally, capable of remaining poised for many months. Their most prominent role is in power projection, either conducting air strikes or supporting amphibious forces. In this context, the British carriers are useful assets for increasingly prevalent joint operations (i.e. those involving more than one service), by virtue of their command and control capabilities, their ability to host a Joint Force Headquarters, and their ability to provide a platform for aircraft operated by the other services, such as *Apache* attack helicopters or RAF *Harriers*.[25] Yet the need for securing sea control should not be overlooked. Since the Falklands War the Royal Navy has undertaken sanctions enforcement (e.g. Iraq, former Yugoslavia), mine clearance (Iran–Iraq War, Gulf War), and protection of both merchant shipping (Iran–Iraq War, Gulf War) and vessels transporting heavy land forces (*Desert Shield*). With the proliferation of modern warships, aircraft, submarines and missiles, securing sea control will continue to be a demanding mission which requires air power for air defence, airborne early warning, anti-submarine and anti-surface warfare, reconnaissance and strike operations. Many future scenarios will involve land-based aviation, particularly maritime patrol or tanker aircraft. Yet to rely wholly on land-based air forces would be to gamble on the unrestricted availability of bases where and when they are needed, and experience both during and since the Cold War suggests that this would be foolhardy. Both during operations in the former Yugoslavia and the uses or threats of force against Iraq since 1991, restrictions have at times been placed on the operation of aircraft from local bases, which resulted in an increased reliance on carrier aviation.

Britain still lacks the luxury of planning to fight major regional conflicts by itself. Nevertheless, there are major UK interests around the world which could entail the deployment of military force, whether in limited-scale national operations or, more probably, in multilateral operations. If a future coalition includes the United States, then the Royal Navy's relative compatibility with the US Navy is a useful asset, as it was in the 1990–91 Gulf conflict. During the crisis, a British carrier was deployed to the Mediterranean to free an American carrier for operations further east. In the Gulf itself, British destroyers and frigates were integrated with the American fleet, escorting high-value US ships, and their *Lynx* helicopters took the lead in eliminating the Iraqi navy.[26] It is difficult to imagine a clearer example of burden sharing. If, on the other hand, a multilateral force does not fully involve the United States, then British naval power and naval aviation take on even more significance, as was shown in the Adriatic, where the UK maintained a carrier for three years in support of UN forces in the former Yugoslavia.[27] British naval aircraft performed a range of tasks in ensuring the security of sea communications, monitoring and then enforcing sanctions and the no-fly zone, supporting troops ashore (not least in providing a contingency force for reinforcement or evacuation) and – the United States by then having taken on the leading role – in the air strikes of Operation *Deliberate Force*. Hence, in terms of possible contributions to multilateral operations, British naval aviation has particular value, which other European allies cannot duplicate as they can with land and air forces. The Royal Navy, with its proven capability to deploy and operate world-wide, offers much to a coalition including the United States and even more to one without them.

Since the end of the Cold War, reductions in the strength of the Royal Navy have fallen on those elements perceived to have less utility in the new environment: thus, the number of submarines has fallen by about half and the number of escorts (particularly anti-submarine) by a quarter. The utility of amphibious forces has been recognised with the commissioning of HMS *Ocean* (a purpose-built helicopter carrier for amphibious operations) and the order of two replacement amphibious assault ships, which also operate helicopters.[28] The carrier force has been maintained at three, although a decision needs to be taken soon about the replacement of both the carriers and the *Sea*

Harrier.[29] On this decision rests the future of the Royal Navy as a significant global actor, able to carry out demanding operations both at sea and from the sea in the face of sophisticated opposition.

Naval aviation is part of a balanced fleet, and provides capabilities that other systems cannot match in securing and exercising the use of the sea, and for power projection. In spite of repeated claims that various technological developments have made carriers obsolete or hopelessly vulnerable, the fact is that although they have seen extensive use in many conflicts, not one has been lost or even seriously damaged since 1945. In reality they have been able to incorporate innovations such as jet aircraft and guided missiles; the same tendency may be predicted for *Tomahawk* land-attack missiles and unmanned aerial vehicles, both of which will become useful complements to manned aircraft, rather than completely replacing them in the near future. Nuclear-powered submarines, the most serious potential threat to carriers, are not in the service of any state that is likely to confront a British task force, and the more widespread conventional submarines are much less of a danger to a properly balanced force.

Naval aviation is expensive to procure and maintain but as the above account has shown, it has proved to be one of the most useful and frequently utilised British military capabilities. The geography and world-wide political and trading interests of the UK naturally turn the country towards naval power, and naval aviation is a fundamental part of a modern fleet; indeed, its possession could plausibly be used as the criterion to distinguish medium from minor navies. Moreover, it is a form of military power that is particularly well suited to the post-Cold War context. Both for Britain's national use and for contributions to multilateral operations, naval aviation represents a unique and valuable asset which greatly expands the options available to policy-makers.

1   This tendency culminated in the Maritime Strategy of the 1980s, for which see "The Maritime Strategy", *US Naval Institute Proceedings*, January 1986 (Supplement); also Norman Friedman, *The US Maritime Strategy* (London, Jane's, 1988).

2   This was recognised by Admiral Sergei Gorshkov, Commander in Chief of the Soviet Navy, who showed a keen awareness of the value of carrier aviation for the Western powers in Korea, Suez, Cuba and Vietnam, and also for broader diplomatic purposes. S.G. Gorshkov, *The Sea Power of the State* (Oxford, Pergamon, 1979), especially pp. 234–45.

3   For the leading exposition of the decline school, see Paul Kennedy, *The Rise and Fall of British Naval Mastery* (Third Edition: London, Fontana, 1991).

4   See, for example, the Chiefs of Staff report, *Defence Policy and Global Strategy*, D (52) 26, 17 June 1952, in CAB 131/12, PRO, London.

5   Norman Polmar notes that US Navy carriers flew some 250,000 operational sorties, with 30,000 from Commonwealth carriers; *Aircraft Carriers* (London, Macmillan, 1969) p. 561. The single British or Australian carrier on station off Korea at any one time carried no more than two dozen *Sea Fury* and *Firefly* fighter/ground attack aircraft.

6   *Statement on Defence 1955 – Cmd. 9391* (1955) paras. 36, 40.

7   *Explanatory Statement on the Navy Estimates 1957-58 by the First Lord of the Admiralty - Cmd. 151* (1957) para. 56. The low level strikes of naval aircraft proved more effective than the RAF's high-level bombing, and carrier aircraft were more responsive and flexible than aircraft based on Cyprus which could only spend ten or fifteen minutes over Egypt; Eric Grove, Vanguard *to* Trident: *British Naval Policy Since World War II* (London, Bodley Head, 1987), pp. 196-97.

8   Memorandum by the Minister of Defence, "Defence Expenditure", D (57) 13, 26 July 1957, in CAB 131/16, PRO, London; para. 6 (b).

9   *Defence: Outline of Future Policy – Cmd. 124* (1957), quotations paras. 37–38.

10 It was noted in 1959 that the three operational carriers "could not be made capable, at any cost, of operating the modern aircraft now in service." *Explanatory Statement on the Navy Estimates 1959–60 by the First Lord of the Admiralty – Cmd. 674* (1959) paras. 11-12.

11 For details of this proposed carrier, see Admiralty Board Memorandum B.1421, "Design of new aircraft carrier to replace HMS *Victorious*", 12 June 1962, in ADM 167/154, PRO, London.

12 *Statement on the Defence Estimates 1966 - Part I: The Defence Review – Cmd. 2901* (1966) especially Chapter II, paras. 2–7.

13 Ibid., para. 4.

14 *Statement on the Defence Estimates – Part II: The Defence Estimates 1966-67, Cmd. 2902* (1966) para. 21; emphasis added.

15 *Supplementary Statement on Defence Policy 1967 Cmd. 3357* (1967) para. 3.

16 Ibid.; *Statement on the Defence Estimates 1968 – Cmnd. 3540* (1968) Chapter I, paras. 1–7.

17 *Cmd. 3357,* Chapter II, paras. 2–4.

18 Ministry of Defence memorandum, in *Expenditure Committee (Defence and External Affairs Sub-Committee) Session 1973–74: Minutes of Evidence Tuesday 22 January 1974: The Cruiser Programme* (London, HMSO, 1974)

19 *Statement on the Defence Estimates 1979 – Cmd. 7474* (1979).

20 *Statement on the Defence Estimates 1981 – Cmd. 8212-I* (April 1981); also House of Commons, *Second Report from the Defence Committee Session 1980–81, Statement on the Defence Estimates 1981* (London, HMSO, 1981).

21 *The United Kingdom Defence Programme: The Way Forward – Cmd. 8288* (1981); for a critical account see Keith Speed, *Sea Change: The Battle for the Falklands and the Future of Britain's Navy* (Bath, Ashgrove, 1982).

22 John F. Lehman, *Command of the Seas* (New York, Scribners, 1988) p. 271.

23 Kenneth Morgan is under the wildly inaccurate impression that the Royal Air Force provided "air cover and defence against air attack"; K. Morgan, *The People's Peace: British History 1945–1990* (Oxford, OUP, 1990), p. 459. In reality, the RAF's role consisted of additional Harriers and helicopters operating from Royal Navy carriers, and the restricted participation of aircraft operating from Ascension.

24 Secretary of State for Defence *The Falklands Campaign: The Lessons – Cmd. 8758* (December 1982) paras. 225, 228. Moreover, two merchant ships used in the conflict were subsequently converted into Royal Fleet Auxiliary helicopter carriers. Grove, op. cit., p. 384.

25 The 1997 "Ocean Wave" deployment to the Far East saw RAF *Harrier* GR7s operate from HMS *Illustrious;* see "RAF discovers its sea legs to stretch Harrier capability", *Daily Telegraph*, 20 March 1997. The provision of such an enhanced strike capability was used in November of the same year in support of diplomatic activity related

to UN arms inspections in Iraq.

26 For an authoritative account of the Royal Navy in the Gulf War, see Captain Chris Craig, *Call For Fire: Sea Combat in the Falklands and the Gulf War* (London, John Murray, 1995).

27 Rear Admiral J.J. Blackham, "Maritime Peacekeeping", *RUSI Journal*, Vol. 138 No. 4. August 1993, pp. 18–23; Eric Grove, "Navies in Peacekeeping and Enforcement: The British Experience in the Adriatic Sea", *International Peacekeeping*, Vol. 1 No. 4, Winter 1994, pp. 462–70.

28 The use of the names *Albion* and *Bulwark* for these ships, just like that of *Ocean* for the LPH, is an appropriate historical choice, since these were the names of the carriers converted into the commando carriers of the 1960s.

29 See Martin Edmonds (ed.), *British Naval Aviation in the 21st Century – Bailrigg Memorandum No. 25* (CDISS, Lancaster University, 1997).

The Future of Submarines

Norman Friedman

During the Cold War, submarine roles, at least as stated, were relatively simple. Western attack submarines were considered the best antidote to Soviet attack submarines which, in wartime, would prey on Western shipping and on Western surface warships. Everyone's strategic submarines helped preserve the peace by maintaining nuclear deterrence. Smaller countries bought submarines largely in hopes of deterring larger ones from making naval attacks (by threatening to sink major units).[1] As for technology, only the major powers had nuclear-powered submarines, though lesser powers wanted them (but could not afford to develop them). Lesser powers had to make do with diesel-powered craft, some of which were operated by most of the major powers, particularly for narrow or shallow waters (and mainly near home). All navies gained access to long-range anti-ship and, usually, anti-submarine homing torpedoes.[2] Many Western navies (and some Third World clients) bought small numbers of submarine-launched anti-ship missiles, principally Sub-*Harpoon*. The Soviets developed their own submarine launched anti-ship missiles, but because these large weapons required special submarines to launch them, they were not exported.[3] Many submarines gained a secondary mine-laying capacity.[4]

Much of this scheme unravelled with the end of the Cold War, yet submarines remain extremely important. That is because the key virtue of the submarine is not its ability to deal with its kind, or to frighten surface sailors, but rather its ability to operate more or less invisibly, in waters whose control is claimed by others. We now know that during the Cold War, for example, many Western submarines spent substantial time near the Soviet coast, collecting intelligence. They also had a vital deterrent role: by proving that they could operate without hindrance (the Soviets did occasionally detect them), they helped convince the Soviet Navy that it could not effectively conduct anti-submarine warfare. That in turn seems to have convinced the Soviets to concentrate scarce naval resources on the protection of the areas in which they planned to operate their strategic submarines, reducing the likely wartime pressure on the open seas.

At the time, much of the intelligence gathered undoubtedly concerned the acoustic signatures of Soviet submarines, data needed to make their later detection surer. Submarines on patrol near Soviet bases would also have been able to detect any major sortie, which might have provided essential warning of a Soviet decision to go to war. Submarines could also conduct essential electronic reconnaissance, to a degree impossible for aircraft or satellites, since they could observe more covertly (radars and radios could be switched off when known electronic reconnaissance platforms were present).

Geography simplified the West's tasks. All of the Soviet bases lay beyond choke points which Western submarines and surface ships could try to close. Those choke points, moreover, lay in or near NATO territory, so transit to them was not onerous.[5]

Now the situation has been transformed. For the next decade or more, the most likely Western naval role is projection of power. It is virtually impossible to predict where naval power will be needed in a very turbulent world, so there is a premium on the sustained mobility of all naval forces. Base structures are unlikely to survive, but even if they did, forward-basing sufficient numbers of ships to cover the whole world will be prohibitively expensive. Similarly, there is surely a premium on the ability to bring the most covert possible collectors of information into play as quickly as possible. Their objectives will include not only local electronic emissions but also mapping out underwater obstacles such as minefields. They will also, of course, want to deny the locals the ability to use their own submarines effectively.[6]

From the point of national policy, the ability to transit covertly may be almost the most valuable one. A submarine can take up station without exacerbating a situation. For example, in 1977 it appeared that Argentina was about to attack the Falklands. British nuclear attack submarines were sent to the South Atlantic as a potential deterrent. The crisis receded, and they came home, never having been detected by the Argentines – and never having inflamed feelings. When a similar crisis began in 1982, the Royal Navy again sent nuclear attack submarines. This time the Argentines went ahead. When that happened, surface ships – public ships – were sent. The submarines of course preceded them. One of them, HMS *Conqueror*, sank the Argentine cruiser *Belgrano*, deterring the Argentine Navy from any subsequent surface activity. British nuclear submarines also took up station off the Argentine coast to report the launch of air raids, so that the task force in the South Atlantic, had sufficient time for reactions. A British diesel submarine landed special forces in the islands themselves.

Today, attack submarines have in *Tomahawk* a highly-accurate, non-nuclear land-attack weapon. It seems likely that in many cases the destruction (or threat of destruction) of a very few key targets can be quite devastating to the ruler of a Third World country, who is often the object of the projection of power. If an air strike is needed, a missile like *Tomahawk* may be able to destroy or paralyse a key air defence centre, making the strike viable.[7] The US Navy demonstrated the missile strike role during the Gulf War.

The extent to which a submarine can directly support surface forces is still an open question. For such operations to be practical, the submarine must be able to communicate freely with the surface force, and vice versa, without giving away its position. For many years that was impossible, largely because of the same factors that give the submarine its effective invisibility. It now appears that, with advances in computers, acoustic communication between submarines and surface forces may indeed become practical in the near future.[8] Because a submarine is generally so well placed to detect other submarines approaching a surface force, direct support has always had considerable appeal – to surface sailors. On the other hand, submariners have always feared that identification errors, which are likely in undersea warfare, would be particularly lethal to any submarine close to the surface force. Easier communication would presumably make for sure identification.[9]

These considerations largely define the desirable characteristics of a post-Cold War submarine operated by a major Western power. It must be able to transit long distances to deal with surprise contingencies, and that long run must not exhaust its crew. Once in theatre, it must be able to conduct self-contained reconnaissance, and it must be able to transmit the fruits of that work back home. It should be able to influence events ashore, at the least by missile attack (and, preferably, by being able to land small units of special forces troops). Beside all this, it ought to be able to fulfil traditional roles such as torpedo attack against surface ships and submarines.

The two choices for submarine propulsion are nuclear (in an SSN) and diesel-electric (in an SSK). The nuclear plant provides virtually unlimited endurance (measured, often, in thousands of hours) at full speed, but at a very high price, both in the purchase of the submarine and in infrastructure.[10] A diesel-electric submarine may approach nuclear speed, but only for a very short time (typically an hour or less), after which its battery must be recharged.[11] That is done by running the diesel, either on the surface or at periscope depth (air is drawn into the submarine via a snorkel). The energy storage capacity of the battery, which is far less than that of chemical fuel, limits a submarine's underwater endurance.

The far more efficient chemical fuel cannot be used by a fully-submerged submarine because the submarine carries no oxidant. Snorkelling is relatively noisy and, therefore, dangerous, to the point that the ratio of time the submarine must snorkel to top up her battery while on patrol is called her 'indiscretion ratio.'[12]

During World War II, the Germans tried to overcome this problem by using hydrogen peroxide as an oxidant, in *Walter* submarines; both Britain and the Soviet Union built experimental *Walter* submarines post-war. They proved dangerous and were abandoned as soon as nuclear power was proven. The Soviets also tried another wartime German idea, a closed-cycle (*Kreislauf*) diesel. In this case the exhaust from a diesel is purged of combustion products and extra oxygen is added before the gas is pumped back into the diesel. The Soviets built an entire class of *Kreislauf* submarines, but found them dangerous.[13] By the time their problems had been solved, nuclear power was far more attractive.

The *Walter* system was intended to provide a diesel submarine with a high burst speed which it could sustain for about ten hours. *Kreislauf* offered something similar, but also protracted low-speed endurance, far beyond what a battery could offer. Current interest in Air-Independent Propulsion (AIP) centres on extending the time the submarine can loiter more or less quietly; it offers sufficient power for speeds of a few knots. Current alternatives include the French MESMA, the German fuel cell, and the Swedish Stirling engine; there is also some interest in reviving *Kreislauf.*

Proponents of AIP may claim two advantages. One is that the submarine may loiter more quietly in an area saturated by anti-submarine forces listening for diesel noise. The second is the possibility of frustrating the standard tactic used against diesel submarines, hold-down. In such operations, surface units simply wait above the submarine until her battery runs down, at which time she must surface to surrender. With AIP, she may be able to creep off at low, silent speed. The main drawback to AIP must be fear that it adds complexity and, perhaps, vulnerability, since the oxidant and fuel may burn.

AIP cannot convert a diesel submarine into a nuclear submarine equivalent. Given the volume of a submarine hull, it seems extremely unlikely that enough fuel and oxidant can ever be carried to do that.[14] Sustained high underwater speed seems to be limited to nuclear craft.

A nuclear submarine enjoys another, more subtle, advantage: more electric power on a sustained basis, to run both active sonars (which may be important in littoral waters) and a more complex combat direction system (which may be essential if a submarine is to make sense of the very complex littoral environment). More power, of course also makes for a better environment inside the submarine, hence for better crew conditions during a long transit. For example, nuclear submarines typically manufacture their own oxygen by breaking down sea water. A diesel submarine forced to remain underwater soon resorts to chemical candles (to generate oxygen) and to chemicals to absorb carbon dioxide, and even these measures cannot be sustained for many days.

Probably the most striking near-term developments are much improved integrated sonar/combat systems and unmanned underwater vehicles (UUVs). As in the case of surface ships, submarines now use computers to assemble a usable picture of activity around them, for example to select which targets to attack. The submarine differs drastically from a surface ship, however, in that her sensors are primarily passive. They give a bearing to a target, but usually not a range. As submarine and target move, target range (and course and speed) can be deduced from the way target bearing changes. Although mathematical techniques exist, in fact bearing and other data are inexact, and typically a human operator intervenes in the calculation. That limits the number of targets most combat systems can realistically handle to something like 20 to 40. That is quite satisfactory in the open ocean; but there may be hundreds of seaborne craft in a littoral area.

Many of the craft (and other sources of noise) can probably be rejected, for example on the basis of signatures; but ideally that should not be necessary. There are two ways out of the problem. One is to automate the target analysis process, perhaps using some form of artificial intelligence. Another is to exploit existing sonar data more completely, in the hope that the combination of data will solve the problem.[15] Given good range data, a tactical picture can be built up, and to some extent reactions to that picture can be automated. For example, in shallow littoral water sonar ranges are often fairly short, so submarines may find themselves encountering others quite suddenly.

Integration means not only forming the tactical picture but also - as in a modern surface warship – almost automatically using that data to fire weapons and countermeasures, and to provide advice needed to evade enemy weapons or detectors. The great object is to allow the submarine commander and weapon officer to focus on the situation, not on the details of how to sense it or how to operate particular weapons. For example, it is clearly desirable that data from different sonars be fused into a single picture. Otherwise, the officers running the submarine must themselves fuse that data, and their concentration on that task is likely to distract them from fighting the ship.[16]

UUVs present many interesting possibilities. For example, the US Navy is currently experimenting with a submarine-launched device which can scout out a possible minefield. Because it is fired from a submarine, and because it operates submerged, the mine detecting UUV can operate entirely covertly. For example, it is not likely to alert an enemy to a potential landing area, as a surface or airborne device would. A submarine might use a UUV for bi-static or multi-static active sonar operation. For example, the UUV could ping, the submarine receiving the echoes. In that way the submarine would avoid the risk of revealing itself by emitting strong sonar signals. For that matter, a short-range UUV might be used to carry antennas and electro-optic sensors, relieving a submarine on surveillance duty from any need to loiter at periscope depth with masts extended.

In the United States, there is also considerable interest in submarine operations using unmanned *air* vehicles (UAVs). If they are small enough, such devices can be launched by means of the same sort of canisters now used to launch anti-ship missiles. Clearly they are one-shot devices, but during their flights they provide the submarine with the vision it may need. For example, during a recent exercise a US submarine used a simulated UAV to support a special forces operation. The UAV found the beach the special forces needed for their landing, it cued them to their target (and observed the results of their raid), and it helped them find their way off the beach and back to the submarine.

New possibilities such as UUVs and UAVs demand more internal volume in a submarine, since the vessel must still stow its numerous weapons. As it is, a submarine has about a third as much internal volume as a surface ship of similar tonnage, so it is always likely to be quite cramped. If indeed the future (at least for the larger navies) favours littoral operations and thus an increased variety of systems, it also seems inevitably to favour the sort of large nuclear-powered submarines now in service. Necessarily smaller diesel or hybrid (with AIP) craft are unlikely to enjoy either the internal volume or the command/control capacity needed.

Littoral operations raise another important point. The submarine will often need more, rather than less, communications capacity. For example, firing a *Tomahawk* at a shore target requires detailed information about not only the target area but also about the path to that area (and preferably about several alternative paths). The results of UUV or UAV reconnaissance may be urgently needed by a battle group commander.

Submariners always distrust communication, because it makes them potentially visible, hence vulnerable. At the least, they will want to be able very quickly to leave the spot from which communication was made. That favours high sustained speed, hence nuclear power.

None of this is to say that nuclear submarines are always ideal, merely to point out that their advantages are key for any navy whose main business is the long-range projection of national power. Clearly nuclear power is expensive. In shallow water, a large nuclear attack submarine may find herself much more constrained than a small diesel-electric boat; but on the other hand, size buys more effective sonars and a better combat direction system, and it may well be relatively easy to modify torpedoes for good shallow-water performance.

Of course there are other important current themes in submarine technology. With advances in computer technology, for example, it is possible to add active silencing (generating sound out of phase with that normally produced by the submarine). In this interesting case, the sound is not completely eliminated; instead, a steerable noise 'spike' is produced, pointed away from an enemy listener. The steer-ability of the spike means that it must be controlled by the same inte-grated combat direction system used to fire weapons.

Another question is whether the shape of submarines ought to change in some radical way. As submarines are currently designed, their prominent fins add considerably to the resistance they experience moving through the water, add to their acoustic signatures, and can cause snap roll, in which a submarine inadvertently dives when she turns (the fins act as a diving plane). Western submarines have those tall fins mainly because of their surveillance missions: masts must be carried above water, and a submarine near the surface is steadiest when her hull is deepest (the height of the fin determines how deep periscope depth can be). With the advent of electro-optical periscopes, there is no longer any need for a tube extending directly into the pressure hull. For example, the sensors might be accommodated on board a pod launched from and then recovered by the submarine, linked to her by an optical fibre. Will we, then, see Western submarines with the very short blended fins that characterise Russian practice? With no fins at all? Or will the other roles of the fin, such as supporting a bridge for manoeuvring in port, and supporting the snorkel of the emergency power plant, keep it in much its present configuration?

Much the same can be said of the currently standard cylindrical hull. Sketches of a proposed Swedish diesel-AIP submarine show a hull more like a flatfish. The object may be merely to operate more effectively near the bottom, but there may also be hydrodynamic advantages.[17]

Whatever its future shape, it seems fair to see in the nuclear attack submarine the ideal complement to surface battle forces in the key naval role of the next few years, and probably of the next few decades, the projection of national and international power into turbulent regions of the world.

1   For some navies, the delivery of special forces and surveillance were more important than torpedo attack. Israel and South Africa probably typify this view, which explains why they have maintained substantial submarine forces despite the fact that neither has ever faced a large hostile surface navy. Cold War secrecy badly distorted the public (or even the internal naval) view of the importance of special operations to the major fleets. For example, only in the last few years has it become clear that the US considered the ability covertly to recover objects from the ocean floor a major Cold War advantage. Several Soviet nuclear submarines were converted to support special submersibles, but their roles remain somewhat unclear (they probably included the wartime destruction of NATO underwater listening devices, which otherwise would have caused the Soviet submarine fleet considerable problems).

3   Often anti-ship and anti-submarine capability are not combined in a single torpedo. However, weapons-carrying capacity is quite limited (often to fewer than 30 weapons), so any requirement to carry many types of weapons can be counterproductive. For example, for a time British submarines had to carry not only the *Tigerfish* homing torpedo (used primarily against submarines) but also the Mk 8 straight-runner (used against surface ships like the Argentine cruiser *Belgrano*). Mk 8 was retired when *Tigerfish* acquired a sufficient anti-ship capability. Often homing torpedoes usable against fast submarines are distinguished from slower ones usable mainly against diesel craft. The rule of thumb is that the torpedo should be 50 per cent faster than the target, so a 30 knot SSN demands a 45 Kiloton (kt) torpedo, whereas a 20 kt SSK can be dealt with by a 30 kt weapon. At least in the past, high torpedo speed was a problem because it increased the noise level at the torpedo seeker. Hence many weapons run out at high (noisy) speed, then slow to search for a target (they may then accelerate again, as long as they can maintain their lock on the target). The distinction between anti-ship and anti-submarine is particularly strong in the Russian case, since anti-ship torpedoes generally home by detecting and following the ship's wake (using an upward-looking sonar), whereas anti-submarine weapons ping directly against the submarine. Note, too, that Russian torpedoes tend to be much longer than their Western counterparts, hence difficult to export to the West and to Western clients. Perhaps the most dramatic torpedo development

of recent times was the revelation about 1993 by the Russians of a straight-running weapon, *Shkval*, capable of attaining 200 kts (it was conceived to be fired back at Western submarines, its nuclear warhead making up for errors in aiming precision).

4   These weapons can be launched by a submerged submarine. At present the only torpedo-tube fired missiles (hence, suitable for export) are the US Sub-*Harpoon* and *Tomahawk* (now in service only in its land-attack version) and the French Sub-*Exocet*. At times the Russians have mentioned a possible submarine-launched version of their Kh-35 (SS-N-25), which broadly resembles the US *Harpoon*. It would indeed be suited to their export submarines. In 1997 the US Office of Naval Intelligence reported that the Chinese were working on a submerged-launch follow-on to their existing *Exocet*-sized C-801.

5   Many submarines can fire mines from their torpedo tubes, the key requirements being that the submarine's fire control system can set the mines and that the torpedo tubes can eject them (many German-built submarines have swim-out tubes that require that anything they launch be self-propelled). In theory, submarines with swim-out tubes can carry specially-designed mine "belts" extending around their pressure hulls, from which mines can be dropped. Despite considerable publicity in Germany and Sweden, however, it does not appear that the "belts" have ever entered service.

6   Hence the Royal Navy's interest in a class of quiet diesel-electric submarines, the *Upholders*, which could operate in the Greenland-Iceland-UK (GIUK) Gap out of bases in Scotland. Of course, when the Soviet Union collapsed this sort of duty was no longer nearly so important; it was more important that all British attack submarines be able to support operations far from home. Hence the demise of the British diesel-electric submarine fleet, despite the youth (and high quality) of the ships involved; their mission had become obsolete.

7   For example, in the Adriatic, Western submarines reportedly kept under surveillance the flotilla of Serbian diesel-electric submarines which threatened the surface ships operating at sea.

8   Clearly, *Tomahawk* can also be carried by surface ships. However, because its launch platform is effectively invisible, a submarine-launched missile enjoys an extra degree of surprise.

9   The great problem was always multi-path: copies, in effect, of the same message travelling along several different paths interfere with each other and parts of the message fade out. Fading can be countered, but normally it drastically limits the rate at which information can be sent. Since the late 1970s there have been attempts to use computers to match the signal to the environment in such a way as to cancel out multi-path. Analogous work in high-frequency radio is already successful in the case of NATO Link 11.

The remaining question is whether the result is covert enough to be acceptable. The usual covert technique, spreading a signal over a wide frequency range, is probably particularly vulnerable to the effects of multi-path.

10   Communications problems also make multi-submarine operations difficult. The Soviets did plan to use groups of submarines, but they simplified matters by limiting themselves to surface targets (using torpedoes which were very unlikely to attack submarines) and also by using a very simplified command vocabulary.

11   In the past, by far the greatest cost of ownership was incurred when a submarine was refuelled. In the 1960s, US submarines were designed to be refuelled twice at eight-year intervals (for a total lifetime of 24 years); the later *Los Angeles*-class is designed for a single refuelling, at about the 15-year mark. The new British *Astute* class and the new US *Seawolf* and New Attack Submarine (NSSN) are designed with one-shot reactors, which will not be refuelled during the submarine's career. By way of contrast, French practice has been to use less-enriched uranium ("caramel"), in the expectation that submarines will be refuelled about every five years (France thus foregoes the expense of an enriched uranium plant). Recent Russian statements suggest that much of their own nuclear submarine fleet has been laid up because no sufficient refuelling infrastructure was ever built up.

12   The fastest diesel-electric attack submarines are rated at about 22 to 24 kts (for one hour). Most are slower. The fastest nuclear attack submarines are about ten knots faster, but some slower ones are limited to about 22 to 25 kts (and some older ones, now retired, were rated below 20 kts). Western nuclear ballistic missile submarines have maximum speeds of about 25 kts.

13   Snorkelling is inherently noisier than running on the surface because all of the diesel's noise goes directly into the water; none goes into the air. Russian-built *Kilo* (Project 877 or 636) class submarines carry short-range air defence missiles (usable only on the surface) in their fins, presumably because they are expected to charge diesels on the surface (where, however, they may be quite recognisable by imaging radar or infra-red detectors). The entire issue of snorkelling noise may be moot. At one time most ships at sea were steam-powered, so a diesel really stood out. Now that diesels are virtually universal, it is difficult to see why a submarine should stand out acoustically. In the Falklands, the commander of the Argentine submarine *San Luis* avoided detection by running inshore, where the sound of surf covered the noise his engines made.

14   Project 615, which NATO called the *Quebec* class; they had three diesels, two of them adapted motor torpedo boat units for high speed sprints. The solution to the fire problem was to develop special hard

nodules which both absorbed carbon dioxide and emitted oxygen. This concept may be applicable to future Air-Independent Propulsion (AIP) projects.

15   In the early 1970s, a US study of a fuel cell submarine showed that a speed of 14 kts could be sustained for about two weeks, given expected (and as yet unrealised) developments in fuel-cell technology. It is conceivable that some radical advance in submarine hull technology, such as a success in using polymers, could drastically reduce resistance and thus increase the maximum speed associated with a given fuel cell. However, it seems unlikely that speed would double on a sustained basis. Nor does it seem likely that fuel cells (or any other closed-cycle power plants) will achieve much more fuel oxidant efficiency than the theoretical figures associated with the US study. The need for power rises as the cube of the speed, so without a change in hull dynamics, a 28 knot fuel cell submarine (comparable to a nuclear submarine), would be using fuel and oxidant at eight times the rate contemplated in the US study. On that basis, the fuel oxidant load used in the study would suffice for less than two days. Enlarging the submarine would somewhat simplify matters (resistance does not rise as quickly as volume), but even a 20 knot two week submarine would probably be quite large.

16   For example, sound bounces off the surface and the bottom. If the elevation/depression angle(s) from which it arrives is automatically measured, and if surface and bottom conditions are known, then a range may be automatically deduced. This sort of performance requires that the sonar, in effect, stare in many directions and at many elevations simultaneously, which imposes a heavy data-processing load – which in turn can now be handled within the volume available, at least on board a good-sized nuclear submarine.

17   Similarly, the ideal combat direction system will always indicate the consequences, not least in noise generated (hence detectability) of alternative courses of action (using, among other things, the same models of sound propagation and underwater topography used in, for example, depression/elevation ranging). Just how well this objective of integration can be achieved within a limited time is not clear.

18   In shallow water (less than operating depth) diesel submarines will bottom when pursued. Nuclear submarines cannot do the same for fear of fouling their condenser inlets, disabling themselves. It is not, however, clear that bottoming offers much advantage to a fast nuclear submarine, whereas it gives a diesel submarine immunity to many forms of attack (torpedoes generally cannot distinguish the submarine from bottom clutter).

Amphibious Operations:
Projecting Sea Power Ashore

Julian Thompson

Sometime in the early 1980s in the wake of defence cuts in the United Kingdom, an alphabetical list of defence or military terminology appeared in the *Times* newspaper, probably penned by a cynical staff officer in the Ministry of Defence. Under the letter 'A' was:

> **Amphibious:** an out of date concept of operations, requiring no particular expertise, which is temporarily undertaken by the Royal Marines.

The quote contains four howlers, but the most glaring is the implication that amphibious operations are the sole preserve of The Royal Marines or any other marine corps. They are but one of the components of the amphibious force; albeit essential. In its turn, the amphibious force of any navy is one of four arms with which maritime warfare can be prosecuted in support of the overall strategy of the state, or group of states. Along with the other three – the surface fleet, submarines, and the air arm – an amphibious force allows the state, or coalition of states, to exercise power not only on, under, and over the ocean, but also on the land that bounds the oceans and seas.

When the threat is easily measured and obvious, it is in theory, possible to tailor one's forces to meet it, arriving at a neat sufficiency; a solution that appeals to anyone who believes that you only need forces to cope with the visible threats at any moment in time. The wise planner rejects this, and even when faced with a known opponent, will build some flexibility into the plans. This is even more important when it is not clear who the next enemy will be; in what form he will appear, and when; because it calls for capability based, rather than threat based maritime forces. Maritime forces are inherently flexible, but their power to project power in all three dimensions – air, sea and land – depends upon possessing an amphibious force; without it, the maritime force concerned can project power in two dimensions only. Further, an amphibious force can poise at sea, it does not have to be committed until the right moment, and in some circumstances the threat to use the force can be sufficient, or it can be employed as a deception, as in the Gulf in 1991, where five Iraqi divisions were kept tied down in positional defence in expectation of a United States Marine Corps landing. An amphibious force can, if the circumstances are right, restore, or speed up, mobility in the land battle by using the sea as the base line from which to provide a turning movement. These and other aspects of amphibious operations will be expanded on later.

At the risk of covering familiar ground, it is important to make clear what is meant by an amphibious operation by explaining what it is not. It is not sea transport. It is not the movement of troops from 'A' to 'B' by sea. This is a common misconception, and those who hold this view will probably ask would it not be easier to take your equipment by sea to a ro-ro harbour, or by air to an airfield, and your troops likewise? It would indeed, if you were sure about two things. First, if you were quite certain where you were going to operate in the future, and therefore knew what facilities existed in those places; and second, if you were confident that a 'red carpet' reception awaited you. Anyone hoping to conduct amphibious operations, should reflect that to do so demands the ability to project a force from sea to land, in a hostile or potentially hostile environment, in a tactical posture, without any reliance on ports and airfields. *Desert Shield*, in Saudi Arabia, was a classic 'red carpet' operation, that is a build-up in a friendly country, which provided three key assets: airfields, ports, and an enormous bonus, fuel; all without any enemy interference whatsoever.

Operations Across the Spectrum of Conflict

Opportunities for conducting Amphibious Operations may present themselves throughout the spectrum of conflict (see Annex A).

Military Operations in Peace

At the lowest intensity end of the spectrum, Military Operations in Peace, it could be thought that conducting *Amphibious* Operations [Author's italics], would be unlikely. However, there are situations where many of the components that go to make up an amphibious capability can be employed with advantage; especially disaster relief, and services assisted evacuation. Examples include the use of amphibious assets, comprising an LPD, landing craft, and helicopters to bring aid to the civil population during the catastrophic floods in the Ganges Delta in what was East Pakistan (now Bangladesh), in 1970; and the recent deployment of forces in Zaire in 1997, standing by to evacuate British nationals. In the former East Pakistan, the devastation caused by the inundation of thousands of square miles of countryside was such that an *Amphibious* Operation was the sole means by which timely relief and succour could be brought to vast numbers of people. Although the forces involved in Zaire were small, and in the event not required, an amphibious asset, the craft and their expert crews were an essential ingredient in the evacuation plan which involved crossing a water gap, the wide Zaire river.

Operations Other Than War

In Operations Other Than War, an amphibious capability can be an adjunct to, or an essential component in, the following:

• Sending a Political Signal

• Evacuation of nationals

• Peacekeeping

• Deterrence

An amphibious force can be deployed off the coast of a country, or region, as a symbol of political will, either in support of, or to bring pressure to bear on, that country or region. Similarly, the amphibious force may be deployed to deter an aggressor about to commit an act of war, or to exert pressure for some other deterrent objective. The utility of an amphibious force during Operations

Other Than War to evacuate nationals, and nationals of friendly countries, is self-evident; including the 'grey area' when others may be fighting, but the UK is not one of the protagonists. For example, the evacuation of British nationals from Kyrenia under the protection of a Royal Marines Commando to an LPH, after the Turkish invasion of Cyprus in 1974.

In a Peacekeeping situation, the peacekeepers may need an entry point secured on the littoral. An amphibious force may be best placed to effect this, particularly if there is a risk of force being employed against the peacekeepers at their disembarkation point, or on their routes inland.

In all the situations discussed above, the amphibious force does not have to be committed until required. As alluded to earlier, it can poise at sea, for several months if need be. The self-sufficiency of a maritime force allows it to dispense with bases. The use of bases, even in friendly or allied territory, may take weeks, or even months, to negotiate, and be hedged about with caveats concerning their use. The stationing of land-based RAF aircraft in Italy in the early days of the peacekeeping operation in the former Yugoslavia, ran into just this kind of problem. Whereas the amphibious force, and accompanying carrier battle group, that spent around four months deployed in the Indian Ocean ready to bring off British and friendly nationals, including US citizens, from Aden in 1967–68, was not inhibited by any considerations involving the sensitivities of basing, or dependency on another's territory.

War Fighting

The employment of Amphibious Forces at the Warfighting end of the spectrum, in Regional Conflict or General War, could include:

- Seizing points of entry for heavier follow-up forces

- Restoring manoeuvre

- Turning operations

- Unlocking the door to the strategic or operational objective

• Deception operations

• Raids

Seiⁱzing Points of ⁱntry for ⁱeavier Folloⁱⁱup Forces

If operations are to be mounted which require the introduction of heavier follow-up forces, but no ports or airfields are available, either because they are held by the enemy or do not exist, amphibious forces can be used to gain a bridgehead into which such forces can be disembarked. If suitable ports and airfields are held by the enemy, it is possible that amphibious forces could be tasked to seize them either by landing directly into the area, or by landing off to a flank, and approaching overland from the beachhead. The landings at San Carlos, and the subsequent land campaign in the Falklands War of 1982, were examples of the use of amphibious forces in the latter role. Although in this case the land campaign was concluded without the introduction of heavier forces, both the ejection of the invaders and the build-up of forces to deter future Argentine aggression required the possession of port and airfield.

ⁱestoring Manoeuvre

If friendly land forces have reached stalemate, and a sea flank is adjacent, an amphibious operation might be the key to restoring manoeuvre. The Allied landings at Anzio in January 1944 were an example of an attempt to do just this, when General Mark Clark's Fifth Army was stalled trying to breach the Gustav line and advance on Rome. Unfortunately, the attempt failed because the landings were not made in sufficient strength to achieve the stated objective, which was to force the Germans to pull out from the Gustav Line, in particular that part covering the route to Rome running up the Liri Valley past Monte Cassino.

Turning Operations

Two classic examples of amphibious turning operations are Termoli in 1943 (a short hook), and Inchon in 1950 (a long hook). The Termoli operation was mounted because Montgomery was concerned that his Eighth Army advancing north from Foggia, up the eastern side of the 'leg' of Italy, would be delayed if the Germans established a defensive position on the Bifurno River. The 2nd Special Service Brigade consisting of 40 (Royal Marines) Commando, Number 3 (Army) Commando, and the Special Raiding Squadron of the SAS carried out a successful amphibious operation at Termoli, outflanking the Bifurno River positions. The advanced guards of the Eighth Army linked up with the 2nd Special Service Brigade within 24 hours.

The long amphibious hook by the 1st United States Marine Division at Inchon, during the Korean War, was the key to forcing the North Korean invaders to retreat north, thus taking the pressure off United Nations forces penned in the perimeter around Pusan, some 250 miles to the south, and allowing them to break out.

Unlocking the Door to the Strategic or Operational Objective

The classic example of the employment of amphibious forces to unlock the door to a strategic objective is provided by the assault on Walcheren Island in 1944. Following the Allied seizure of Antwerp, so badly needed for logistic supply, all efforts to open up the River Scheldt to traffic were frustrated by the shore batteries on the island of Walcheren lying in the mouth of the estuary. The batteries were captured by three Royal Marines commandos of 4th Special Service Brigade, landing at Westkapelle.

Deception Operations

An amphibious force can play a deception role, by its very existence and by posing a threat to land. The most recent example at the operational level has been alluded to already the deception practised by United States amphibious forces in the war against Iraq in 1991. At a strategic level, extensive forces can be kept pinned down to defending long stretches of coastline by the threat of an amphibious operation.

Raids

Raiding, either as part of deception operations or in support of main force operations, is another of the capabilities provided by an amphibious force. History provides numerous examples, such as the Royal Marine Commando attacks on the coastal railways in North Korea during the Korean War, and the destruction of Argentine aircraft on Pebble Island by an SAS squadron launched from a destroyer in Royal Navy helicopters. The SAS squadron were at the time part of the landing force for the Falklands operation.

Requirements for Amphibious Operations

Clearly, in order to play the 'amphibious card' certain conditions need to be met, mostly in the form of assets. Overarching all these is political will, and an understanding by governments of amphibious operations in the broadest sense.

Shipping

As far as hardware is concerned, the first priority is specialised shipping, without this *amphibious* operations, as defined at the start of this chapter, are impossible. Apart from any other considerations, correctly designed amphibious shipping will allow last minute changes to be made to the plan to meet a changing situation ashore. A mix of shipping is required, consisting of helicopter carriers with a full length deck, ships with wet docking facilities (wet docks), and roll-on-roll-off vessels (ro-ros).

First, carriers: the assault helicopter carrier (in the jargon Landing Platform Helicopter or LPH), is a minimum requirement. Although in an ideal world more flexibility is provided by a ship which combines a full length helicopter deck and wet dock, the UK LPH, with deck only, and some small landing craft carried at davits is more attainable within foreseeable financial constraints. The purpose-built LPH, optimised to carry troops has considerable advantages over a conventional carrier used in this role. Doing so is usually at the expense of all or part of the primary role of the carrier, and troops thus carried in cramped conditions suffer degradation of their operational efficiency on all but short transits. It is also important to remember that the LPH on its own can land only a lightly equipped force with little combat power, limited to taking on light opposition in a short time frame, in a tactical situation where expenditure rates of ammunition and other logistic items is low. To fight a well equipped enemy in a sustained all-arms battle demands the ability to lift heavier equipment and supplies. This requires at least three other types of ship.

Wet docks are best provided by ships like the present and proposed UK assault ship (Landing Platform Dock or LPD). The ship floods its dock, and by opening its tailgate, craft can take loads from within the ship to and from the beach. 'Ro-ro' facilities are provided by ships like the UK Landing Ship Logistic or LSLs. To land a brigade sized force, with some artillery, no armour and a bare minimum of logistic support would require the following:

one LPH(800)

one LPD(500)

four LSLs(4x350)

Even at overload the brigade is well under 3,000 strong. So if more than light opposition is expected, a sizable back-up of a third type of ship, merchantmen, is needed to make the force logistically viable.

Ship–shore Movement

Complementary to the shipping are the ship-shore movement assets: helicopters, landing craft, small craft and hovercraft. Without these the force can neither be landed nor supported ashore.

Helicopters

Using a UK example, a working minimum helicopter allocation for a brigade size force would be:

6 x Lynx helicopters armed with anti-tank missiles

12 x Gazelle helicopters for reconnaissance/command and control

24 x Sea King medium lift helicopters (or equivalent lift in *Merlin* helicopters)

The medium lift helicopter force given above would lift two company groups in one wave, a total of 300 men with some support weapons and ammunition. Clearly it is desirable to have a true attack helicopter, to replace the *Lynx* which is a utility helicopter with a button-on anti-tank system. All helicopters should be 'marinised', that is optimised for operating at sea.

Landing Ships and Craft

A range of landing craft is necessary to lift heavier loads, armoured vehicles, logistic supplies, and a large number of troops at one time. Smaller craft should be capable of loading at the davit head, and larger craft should be carried in the wet dock.

LSLs can beach, or lower stern or bow ramps to craft or pontoons. This is very much second-best to docking, because sea-state limitations are much lower. Sea state will have an even greater effect on craft loading or discharging at merchant ship ro-ro ramps. The MEXEFLOTE which can be assembled into a 60 or 120 foot raft driven by large outboard engines, is a valuable force multiplier, able to load and discharge quickly. It can be carried lashed on to the side of an LSL or in pieces on deck.

Hovercraft or landing craft air cushion (LCAC) are another force multiplier, because of their ability to dispense with double handling of loads at the water-line, and delivering troops close to the objective, provided the terrain inland is suitable.

Finally, there is a need for small craft for raids and special operations including rigid raiders, rigid inflatables, inflatables, and canoes.

Command and Control

The success of an amphibious operation depends heavily on the quality of its command and control arrangements. At any level from commando/ battalion to division and up, there will be at least two headquarters involved in planning and executing the landing and subsequent operations – those of the landing force commander, and the commander of the amphibious group – that is up to the moment that the amphibious operation is deemed to have finished, when command devolves solely on to the landing force commander. There could also be an in-theatre commander, carrier battle group commander, and a joint commander. Hence the need for specialised command facilities on board one of the ships in the amphibious group.

Naval Gunfire Support

The guns of the Navy's ships lying offshore may be necessary to provide fire support:

• Before and during the run-in by troop-carrying helicopters and landing craft.

• While the build-up ashore is in progress, before the landing force artillery is landed.

• To augment landing force artillery fire missions on targets that are within range of ships on the gunline at sea.

Air Support

In most circumstances the amphibious force will need support from a range of aircraft types including: Close Air Support (CAS), particularly for the landing force against ground targets, Airborne Early Warning (AEW), Anti-submarine Warfare (ASW), Anti-surface Warfare (ASuW), and Air Defence (AD). These aircraft can either be organic to the amphibious force, or more probably carried in a separate escort or covering force, which ought to include a carrier group.

The Landing Force

Last, but not least, the Landing Force must comprise fit, well trained and motivated troops, equipped with modern weapons. They, and their leaders and formation and unit staffs, should be thoroughly conversant with all aspects of amphibious operations. This requires training and practice. It will be too late to acquire these skills if mounting an amphibious operation at short notice.

Conclusion

Amphibious forces enable a maritime power, either alone or in concert with allies, to project sea power ashore in a range of contingencies, across the spectrum of conflict. The force can be tailored to meet the situation it is likely to face. The force can be independent of bases and shore facilities. It does not have to be deployed ashore until the time is ripe. It is not reliant on airfields and ports to effect an entry. It can either operate on its own to land a force, or as the forerunner of a larger force, or to the flank of a main force operation. Correctly configured and operating with other maritime forces, an amphibious force can land troops and equipment on a potentially hostile shore, and support subsequent operations ashore. No other force confers such flexibility.

THE SPECTRUM OF CONFLICT – Annex A

		CONFLICT OTHER THAN WAR	WAR	
			REGIONAL CONFLICT	GENERAL WAR
CONDITIONS	PEACE			
RESPONSE	MILITARY OPS IN PEACE	OPS OTHER THAN WAR	WAR FIGHTING	

NUCLEAR DETERRENCE FROM THE SEA

Eric Grove and Lee Willett

According to current British maritime doctrine, 'the maintenance of a secure strategic nuclear deterrent is the first Military Task of the Royal Navy.'[1] Nuclear weapons provide Britain with considerable political and strategic reach when deployed in nuclear-powered submarines. The nature of the sea, as a medium that covers most of the world's surface and one largely impermeable to electro-magnetic radiation, makes it an excellent place to deploy one's nuclear forces covertly and distantly. Ballistic missile-firing submarines (SSBNs) carrying submarine-launched ballistic missiles (SLBMs) are the ultimate guarantors of nuclear deterrence and, more importantly, national security. Hard to detect and safer from counterforce action than land-based forces, SSBNs have, for three decades, provided Britain with a secure, long-range nuclear strike capability to deter aggression by holding at risk objects of value in the homeland of a possible aggressor.[2]

The first SLBMs were relatively inaccurate and inflexible weapons, only useful for massive countervalue retaliation against soft targets. Even with the highly accurate inertial navigation systems developed for the submarines of the 1960s it proved impossible at first to give SLBMs the precision of their land-based counterpart. Also, command and control was much more difficult: sending complex targeting orders to submarines was harder than it was to shore-based forces. Against a state with powerful surveillance and naval capabilities (such as the Soviet Union) it was inadvisable for an SSBN to fire less than its entire load in a strike. Hence SLBMs were considered to be systems of assured destruction. In addition, their deployment by the super powers as contributors to strategic stability was encouraged by the US-Soviet Strategic Arms Limitation Talks (SALT) and Strategic Arms Reduction Talks (START) treaties.[3]

MARITIME POWER AND BRITISH DETERRENCE POLICY: FROM POLARIS TO SUB-STRATEGIC TRIDENT

Historically, the Royal Navy had been in two minds about SSBNs: this was largely because of the raw fiscal costs involved and the resulting likely impact on other programmes. When first appraised of the *Polaris* concept by the United States, the Admiralty saw the advantages of a British SLBM force as a more effective minimum deterrent than the existing *Vulcan* bombers, but did not wish to divert resources from the power projection navy, based on carriers, to which it was committed. The Admiralty perceived that an attempt to take over the strategic bombardment role would encourage – perhaps force – the RAF to mount a serious attack on the carrier force. Hence the RN was happy to see *Skybolt* missiles ordered to lengthen the life of the *Vulcan* bombers long enough for the carrier programme to be secured. Then the time would be ripe for *Polaris*. This plan foundered on American cancellation of *Skybolt* and the need to go for *Polaris* as the only real remaining option. The results were as the Admiralty had feared. The financial effects of *Polaris* were mitigated by agreement to meet extra costs at least in part from central funds, but the RAF duly mounted an attack on the carriers, and this eventually succeeded.

The UK adopted a policy of minimum deterrence, resting on the possession of a small squadron of four SSBNs, of which one would always be at sea, ready to destroy major urban centres in the USSR should the UK suffer nuclear attack. This reflected the adoption of the 'Moscow Criterion', the requirement that Britain should be able to destroy Moscow, the centre of Soviet power and thus of fundamental value to the Soviet leadership. The *Polaris* A-3, the UK's chosen missile, delivered in its original version three 200 kiloton (KT) warheads in a closely spaced, although not especially precise, cluster. The modified Chevaline version reportedly gave the ability to deliver 32 warheads and a large number of balloon decoys, thus swamping Moscow's Anti-Ballistic Missile (ABM) defences.[4]

When *Polaris* replacement was being considered at the end of the 1970s, the 'Moscow Criterion' was a paramount planning assumption. It stood somewhat uneasily both with the argument that British SSBNs provided a second centre of decision-making in NATO and that British forces allocated to the Alliance (except when fundamental national interests were at stake) would have been capable of credible escalation in Europe. For these reasons some analysts advocated replacement and improvement of the RAF's nuclear strike capacity rather than a new generation of SSBNs. These thoughts were also stimulated by Royal Navy fears of the costs of a new SSBN programme.[5]

However, there appeared to be no better strategic, political *and* economic option than the American *Trident* programme.[6] *Trident* in its C-4 variant was perceived at the time as the most credible, and cheapest, way of fulfilling the 'Moscow Criterion' against the expected level of Soviet ABM defences of the late 1990s and the next millennium. Many other options were seen as too costly, particularly given Britain's relatively weak overall economic position. For example, another of the most noted options, the nuclear-armed *Tomahawk* land-attack cruise missile (TLAM/N), would have needed to have been deployed in very large quantities to bring a similar capability: it was officially estimated that anywhere between 11 and 17 TLAM-armed SSNs would have been required.[7] In July 1980 the Thatcher government took the decision to purchase *Trident* from the US, the costs of which would be borne by the RN.

Then came another unilateral American decision with significant repercussions for British deterrence policy. The Reagan Administration decided to concentrate on the upgraded *Trident* D-5, and to phase out the C-4 earlier than originally planned. *Trident* D-5 was a MIRVed (Multiple Independently-Targeted Re-entry Vehicle), highly accurate counterforce weapon designed to give the US SLBM force the precision and discrimination of the US Air Force's (USAF) Intercontinental Ballistic Missiles (ICBMs). One implication of the US decision was that, on existing plans, Britain would be left as it had been with *Polaris*, trying at great expense to maintain a system no longer deployed by the US.[8] There seemed to be little alternative for Britain but to go for the D-5, despite its characteristics appearing over-designed for British political and strategic purposes at the time. On 11 March 1982 it was announced that the UK had opted for the improved D-5. Within this programme, the decision not to maintain a separate national stockpile of missiles (using instead the USN facility at King's Bay, Georgia) and the re-phasing of the programme allowed savings that ensured the survival of other RN assets.[9] However, the *Trident* D-5 still seemed to be, as the then First Sea Lord Sir Henry Leach put it, a 'cuckoo in the nest.'[10]

The decisions of the 1980s have been vindicated in the 1990s in a rather strange and ironic way. The Moscow Criterion seems of much less importance in the post-Cold War world. However, the uncertainties within modern Russia, Moscow's adoption of a greater emphasis on nuclear capabilities in its current military doctrine and, not least, its continued possession of a superpower-standard nuclear striking force make advisable Britain's retention of a national means of effective retaliation. With the political climate effectively undermining the credibility of counter-city and -population targeting, today the C-4 (although still in service in the post-Cold War US strategic nuclear arsenal and cheaper than the D-5) could not provide Britain with the highly precise, discriminating, point-targeting deterrent the UK now needs and which the D-5 provides. The D-5 is probably the most flexible, cost-effective post-Cold War nuclear force for Britain.[11]

Sub-Strategic Trident

However, the end of the Cold War has precipitated substantial changes in British nuclear deterrence strategy. Britain is today able to achieve credible deterrence with lesser nuclear forces. When the WE177 *Tornado*-launched warhead is retired in 1998, *Trident* will be Britain's only deployed nuclear asset.[12] Moreover, nuclear weapons across the NATO spectrum are also being withdrawn. With this, the retirement of the WE177 and *Trident*'s variable warhead package in mind, the RN will progressively subsume the Royal Air Force in Britain's 'sub-strategic' nuclear deterrent role as well as taking a greater weight of NATO's sub-strategic deterrent burden.[13]

Sub-strategic nuclear deterrence is the flexible capacity 'to deliver more limited nuclear attacks than that maintained for strategic nuclear deterrence[,] to provide nuclear deterrence in circumstances in which the threat of strategic nuclear attack may not be credible.'[14] The key aspect of the sub-strategic concept is that the focus of use of nuclear force in this context centres on action significantly short of the ultimate threat of strategic nuclear use, but action still sufficient to deter or coerce an aggressor.[15] Its passive or active use can be both for military effect and, politically, to threaten further escalation in both deterrent and coercive contexts.[16] 'Sub-strategic' is a strategic and political concept and a policy only. It is not a military capability, nor is it a war-fighting strategy[17]. Moreover, in theory it does not dilute the effectiveness of the broader strategic deterrent in any way.

The sub-strategic concept developed as part of the evolution of nuclear strategy, deterrence and Flexible Response. It retains strategic and political power, utility and credibility that were as relevant during the Cold War as they are today. In the modern world, the threat of the use of sub-strategic nuclear force is an integral part of NATO's nuclear strategy, and the assignment of Britain's sub-strategic assets to NATO continues Britain's contribution to Alliance burden-sharing. Britain's role as a deterrent force is growing because of US cuts in its strategic arsenal, particularly in its own *Trident* capability. Along with the French independent deterrent, Britain's *Trident* force provides Europe with options additional to those provided by the US.

Trident in strategic and sub-strategic mode provides Britain with a capability flexible enough to meet the situation in hand. Thus today, nuclear deterrence still plays a key political and strategic role. The 'sub-strategic' rationale, however, perhaps needs further thought. This is largely because, today, Britain is faced with having to deter adversaries other than the former Soviet Union: these adversaries can threaten Britain with several different weapons of mass destruction and, more crucially, do not share the same conception of deterrence as developed by and between NATO and the Warsaw Pact over 40 years. The most likely scenario for the use of deterrence or limited nuclear force is against rogue states threatening the use of weapons of mass destruction against deployed British forces or other targets of British interest. 'Sub-strategic' *Trident* is a more appropriate, and credible, political and strategic counter-threat in these 'new', volatile and unpredictable scenarios.[18]

Analysis of the sub-strategic concept has been evident in military and academic circles, if not in official government documentation. However, the continuing emphasis on a sub-strategic capability reflects the new Labour government's election manifesto commitment to develop a defence policy which more accurately reflects the strategic order in the modern world.[19] It is arguable that the public emphasis placed on the 'sub-strategic' concept has merely served to provide nuclear force with a political rationale and strategic credibility in this new world order. Today, though, particularly with the Strategic Defence Review (SDR) in mind, cost-effective weapons head the political agenda. In the context of the requirements of nuclear deterrence and the perceived threats to British security, a sub-strategic policy provides at the very least a politically cost-effective solution.

TRIDENT, NEW LABOUR AND THE STRATEGIC DEFENCE REVIEW

It is apparent that the government is seeking, through SDR, to place its own clear mark on British defence policy within the context of more accurately reflecting British defence requirements. It is thus likely that SDR will bring some major policy and force structure changes. *Trident* has apparently been 'ring-fenced' from SDR. However, parallel to SDR there is a review of nuclear strategy. Thus, although the *Trident* programme itself may be exempt from SDR, British nuclear strategy generically may instead come under review. This may mean broader, indirect policy and operational adaptations which directly affect Britain's *Trident*/strategic deterrent capability. No decision has yet been made on the SDR and wider nuclear strategy debates. However, should *Trident* be involved in this way, there are four possible areas of focus.

First, and perhaps the most central question, is whether Britain still needs to maintain a continuous deterrent at sea. A key issue here is the required state of readiness. It is arguable that there is perhaps not a need to have the SSBNs on such a deployment cycle, and that such patterns can be adapted without decreasing the state of readiness required in today's new strategic context. If the relationship with Russia remains relatively benign and no other credible missile threat to Britain emerges, then perhaps there is no need to have an SSBN on patrol at all times.[20] In today's political context, Britain's deterrent capability could be used more overtly than in the past. For example, depending on the situation in hand, it may on some occasions make sense in crisis management terms to sail an SSBN with some publicity, perhaps while another is already at sea. There is, however, an argument that such a move could be viewed as escalatory: the public sailing of a nuclear boat would tell an aggressor that the UK intended to use nuclear weapons if UK wishes were not observed. The key factors

116

here are possessing, demonstrating and communicating to the adversary the commitment, capability and intent to use force, but in a credible manner: selecting force levels commensurate to the situation is essential if Britain is not to be self-deterred.

However, a radical policy decision such as ending the continuous deterrent patrols has more far-reaching implications for British security: a retraction of Britain's permanent deterrent could indicate that Britain was withdrawing from its wider global commitments and, in particular, that the RN was no longer a global force. The government has already asserted that Britain's foreign policy will be internationalist, not isolationist.[21] Also, *if* such a decision is on the agenda, then it should be carefully considered, in broader political terms, because of the signal that the public withdrawal of Britain's biggest 'stick' might send to a potential aggressor. Certainly, the end of the Cold War does not mean the end of the potential threats to British security.

Second, with changing strategic criteria in mind, there may be scope to change the weapons packages of the *Vanguard*-class boats to give the *Trident* programme as a whole more credible political and military utility. However, there are other military options that could be considered for *Trident*. *Tomahawk* conventional and, even, nuclear systems, for example, would give *Trident* the role of a quasi-strategic deep-strike arsenal ship.[22]

Third, another option might be to operate the *Vanguard*-boats like more other warships, without the expense of two crews. The government remains committed to the procurement of the fourth boat of the class. However, the on-going need for four-boat fleet and for two crews per boat are subjects that have been widely debated in political, military and academic circles for some time. Operating alternatives more frequently postulated in the academic world for the fourth *Vanguard* boat include using it without its complement of missiles, such as for training and storage purposes, or else mothballing it, bringing it out in times of need. It must be stressed, though, that these options are not feasible, or desirable, while Britain remains committed to a continuous deterrent cycle, a commitment for which four boats are required. Under the Long-Term Costing (LTC) reviews of the early 1990s, it was decided that the *Vanguard* boats would ultimately have to operate with single, augmented crews.[23] However, it is arguable that if crew levels are reduced *without* adapting patrol patterns and lengths accordingly, this may create personnel problems both with regard to current levels of morale and future levels of recruitment.

Last, programme costs and commitments could be adapted by allocating fewer warheads to each missile. Current policy is that each *V*-boat will carry no more than 96 warheads.[24] The Ministry of Defence has previously stated that the missiles might be fitted 'possibly with significantly fewer' warheads than this.[25] The current Labour government has stated that it will retain *Trident*. However, although possibly under the nuclear strategy review (as opposed to SDR itself), Defence Secretary George Robertson has made it clear that the government *will* examine the issue of warhead numbers.[26] It has been suggested that the government may be considering fitting the D-5s with the warhead capacity of the *Polaris*/Chevaline package, *ie.*, a two-warhead, non-MIRV capability.[27] This, however, coupled with the withdrawal of the WE177, arguably would undermine Britain's broader strategic needs, even if the overall deterrent cycle was altered.

Such arguments, though, may not be representative of the type and extent of change that the government is seeking under SDR. It is also important to note that the British *Trident* programme is assuming greater political and strategic significance in relation to both British and US force structures: the withdrawal of the WE177 means that *Trident* will soon be Britain's only nuclear asset; the US plans to retire its first four *Ohio*-class *Trident* SSBNs from their deterrent role means that the British *Trident* capability represents a larger percentage of the West's deterrent arsenal. Such growing importance may afford Britain a greater degree of influence in a variety of political equations, influence it might not wish to relinquish as yet by restricting the *Trident* programme. Also, in today's fluctuating political environment, the continuously-available *Trident* remains a very useful deterrent. Despite the debate at the time of writing over its future role, *Trident* remains a key element at the top-end of the RN's power projection spectrum ranging from conventional cruise missile-equipped SSNs through to aircraft carriers and amphibious forces.

1   *BR1806: The Fundamentals of British Maritime Doctrine.* Directorate of Naval Staff Duties, Royal Navy. D/DNSD 8/36. 1995. London, HMSO. p. 83. The BR1806 definition was drawn from the 1995 *Statement on the Defence Estimates* (from the section on Military Tasks, 1.1 & 2.1). For a similar definition, see: MOD. *Statement on the Defence Estimate 1996.* Command 3223. London, HMSO. pp.23–4 & 56.

2   *BR1806.* Ibid., p. 237.

3   SALT and START focused on land-based ballistic nuclear systems. Thus, mirroring the 'balloon' theory, arms control reductions in one area arguably inspired increased deployments in others. In this case, reductions in land-based strategic forces encouraged the development and deployment of more substantial and capable SLBM/SSBN (and nuclear and conventional SLCM) forces.

4   By inference, thus, Chevaline meant that 16-tube *Polaris* SSBNs would carry missiles fitted with two warheads apiece.

5   It has been argued that, ultimately, the *Polaris* programme proved to be remarkably inexpensive (see, for example: L. Freedman, 1989. *The Evolution of Nuclear Strategy.* International Institute for Strategic Studies: Studies in International Security no.20. London: MacMillan. p.312).

6   Freedman. *Ibid.,* p.312, incl.*n25.*

7   For discussion, see Willett, L. 'Strategic Choice and Coercive Force in the Modern World: the Royal Navy and the Use of TLAM in Support of Policy and Operations.' Forthcoming.

8   For discussion on this point (including its parallels to the *Skybolt/Polaris* debate) see Freedman, L: (1980). *Britain and Nuclear Weapons.* London: MacMillan; (1989). *The Evolution of Nuclear Strategy.* pp.309-12.

9   Such assets included HMS *Fearless* and HMS *Intrepid.*

10   First Sea Lord Sir Henry Leach. 'Britain's Maritime Forces: the Future.' Lecture to the Royal United Services Institute, 9 June 1982. Reproduced in *RUSI Journal,* September 1982. p.13. Cited in Grove, E. (1987). Vanguard *to* Trident: *British Naval Policy since World War II.* London: the Bodley Head Press/Annapolis, MD: US Naval Institute Press. p.350, incl.*n24.*

11   Today, the developing submarine and ballistic missile capabilities of many other nations provide key potential threats to Britain's national security. The added stealth of the *Vanguard-*class *Trident* SSBNs and the greater range and sophistication of the D-5 itself both help ensure the continued effectiveness of Britain's deterrent.

12 In political terms, the deployment of Britain's ultimate weapon of deterrence on a sea-based platform is arguably the best option given the possible absence of the host nation support facilities required to support the use of the WE177-carrying *Tornados.*

13 For reference, see: *BR1806.* p.83; MOD. *Statement on the Defence Estimates* 1996. pp.24 & 56; interviews (conducted for the authors' wider research on British maritime power); Oman, D. 1996. 'Nuclear Deterrence in a Changing World: the View from a UK Perspective', in *RUSI Journal,* vol.141, no.3. June 1996. p.18. Within the *Trident* programme, Britain makes its own warheads and submarines: the US produces the missile, guidance and MIRV technology. Britain's *Trident* warhead was initially reported to have a 150 kiloton yield (Rogers, P. 1988. *Guide to Nuclear Weapons.* Bradford Peace Studies Papers: New Series no.2. New York: St. Martin's Press). It is known that Britain's *Trident* fleet can carry variable numbers of warheads per missile. However there may be other aspects of the capability, such as warhead yield, which can also vary (for reference, see: Oman. 1996. 'Nuclear Deterrence in a Changing World.' p.20; *Hansard.* 12 March 1997. vol.292, no.80. col.188; *Jane's Fighting Ships 1997-98.* Surrey: Jane's Information Group. 1997. p.755; 'Interview with David Clark.' *Jane's Defence Weekly,* vol.27, no.4. 29 January 1997. p.32).

14 *BR1806.* pp.237-8 (see also p.83).

15 See, for example: Rogers, P. (1996). *Sub-Strategic* Trident: *a Slow-Burning Fuse.* London Defence Studies, no.34. Centre for Defence Studies, King's College, London. London: Brassey's. p.4.

16 Deterrence and coercion can be both active and passive. For discussion, see Willett. 'Strategic Choice and Coercive Force in the Modern World'. Forthcoming.

17 The missiles will not necessarily receive any less numerous or less powerful warheads, nor will the SSBNs themselves be undertaking different patrol patterns and sectors. Certainly, it should be noted that 'sub-strategic' does *not* (necessarily) mean single warhead.

18 Arguably, the retaliatory use of nuclear weapons against states using such weapons would be legally and morally justified: the massed use of chemical or biological weapons would forfeit the benefit of the assurances of non-use of nuclear weapons given by the nuclear weapon states as part of the Non-Proliferation Treaty (NPT) process. Also, many academic and military sources have argued that, in the 1991 Gulf War, Saddam Hussein was deterred from using chemical and/or biological warfare by the possibility that the US would respond with tactical nuclear weapons: this was widely perceived to be the case because of the sizeable presence of Coalition nuclear forces in the Gulf in 1991 (for discussion on this latter point, see: Rogers. (1996). *Sub-Strategic* Trident. pp.28-33; *The Observer,* 6

January 1991. *Trident* could be fired either as a single demonstration shot or else on a much wider scale, such as a pre-emptive strike against an aggressor. The danger of such 'rogue' states mistaking a limited Trident strike for a massive 'strategic' attack would not arise nor would the submarine be endangered by the launch giving away its position as such states do not have sophisticated ocean surveillance and early warning devices.

19   See: The Labour Party. *Because Britain Deserves Better.* April 1997. p.38.

20   Given today's general alert state, perhaps a more viable political, strategic and fiscal strategy for *Trident* operations would be to have a four-boat operational role concept designed as follows (weapons loads would probably be tailored for the mission concerned): first, one role as the nominated strategic deterrent (this boat should be ready to sail at 24 hours notice); second, another role as the nominated 'sub-strategic' deterrent; third, a boat on stand-by as a trouble-shooter (this boat would be ready to sail at 48 hours notice); it is assumed that the fourth boat would be in re-fit or on work-up.

21   McInnes, C. (1997). *'Meet the New Boss: Same As the Old Boss'?. Labour's Strategic Defence Review 1997-8.* Paper presented to the British International Studies Association (BISA) annual conference, Leeds, 15-17 December 1997. p.8. McInnes cited a quotation from Hon George Robertson, in which the Secretary of Defence stated that Britain is 'internationalist not isolationist.' (p.8).

22   The US Navy has been considering such an option for quite some time. First, it converted the *Benjamin Franklin*-class SSBNs USS *Kamehameha* and USS *James K. Polk* into special forces delivery systems. Second, more recently it has been giving serious consideration to converting the first four *Ohio*-class SSBNs (which carry the C-4 *Trident)* into *Trident/Tomahawk* strike platforms, rather than retiring them. Also, proposals for developing an altogether new arsenal ship have been dropped. (For more recent discussion on the US debate, see: Carey, M. 'Give *Tridents* a New Role: Decommissioned Subs Offer Conventional Punch', in *Defense News*, 24-30 November 1997. p.23; Courter, J. 'The Boomer Reborn', in *Proceedings*, vol.123/11/1, 137. United States Naval Institute. November 1997. pp.51-3). Given that two central aspects of today's politico-military agenda are sub-strategic nuclear options and the use of military force at a lower cost, nuclear TLAMs might be an option worth considering.

23   These crews, however, will be slightly larger than the standard 150 personnel currently serving on each of the four boats' two crews. In fact, they may be up to 25% larger.

24   Each *Trident* missile is technically capable of carrying 12 warheads, thus giving each *V*-boat a maximum warhead capacity of 196.

25   MOD. (1996). *Statement on the Defence Estimates* 1996. p.56.

26   See: Chalmers, M. *British Nuclear Weapons Policy: the Next Steps.* International Security Information Service. May 1997.

27   Key members of the current government have hinted at this in the past. Foreign Secretary Robin Cook, for example, wrote in *The New Statesman* in April 1995 that, as a first step in an eventual freeze on nuclear warhead numbers, 'Britain should announce that it will deploy no more warheads on *Trident* than are currently deployed on *Polaris*' (Cook, R. 'Bombs Away: UK Nuclear Non-Proliferation Policy', in *The New Statesman & Society*, vol.8, no.342. 14 April 1995).

Coercion from the Sea

Michael Codner

'Coercion' did not appear in official NATO documents and papers during the Cold War.[1] The use of the word would have made European Allies quail and would have reinforced the worst fears of the Soviet Union. In the post-Cold War era, however, 'coercion' has been much discussed. Indeed, there is something of a fashion for the word in British defence circles.

Current British military doctrine distinguishes coercion from deterrence. It sees deterrence as 'essentially a passive function'. Coercion on the other hand 'moves deterrence onto an active and more focused plane by the direct threat of the use of force in a measured way, not as an act of conflict or to achieve a military objective, but in order to compel a particular course of action'.[2] However one of the contentions of this chapter is that the 'active' versus 'passive' relationship between coercion and deterrence is not perhaps as simple as it seems.

It was during the Cold War that the diplomat, Sir James Cable, published his classic works on gunboat diplomacy[3], a very large class of naval operations whose purpose was to alter the behaviour of target governments. He did not use the word 'coercion'. What diplomat would? But his categories of 'definitive', 'purposeful', `catalytic' and 'expressive' gunboat diplomacy broadly lay within its modern definition.

In 1993 a paper by the Naval Staff on conventional deterrence[4] analysed the use of limited force in situations other than extended combat to modify the behaviour of target governments and leaderships. This paper argued that deterrence needed to be redefined to reflect the changed strategic environment. Deterrence could not be specifically focused on the residual Russian threat and the prevention of invasion of allied territory - nor was it dependent on linkage to nuclear weapons. Needless to say, the paper was highly controversial for the suggestion that in most operational situations the threat of nuclear escalation would not be an option. It concluded that Britain and her Allies would be obliged to rely on an inherently more risky concept of conventional deterrence in protecting their interests. The paper went on to argue that deterrent action in the emerging strategic environment is best understood as part of a wider concept of 'armed suasion.'[5]

The idea that truculent governments and leaderships might be effectively coerced was subsequently coupled with the successful bid for *Tomahawk* cruise missiles for the Royal Navy's nuclear attack submarines. 'Coercion' emerged into the public domain in a speech by the then Secretary of State for Defence in 1994.[6] More recently the coercive use of airpower has been much explored by analysts in connection with attempts to bring Saddam Hussein to heel after the Gulf War of 1991 and to cajole the Bosnian Serbs in the period leading up to the Dayton Peace Accord.[7]

This gallop through recent history is important because it exposes the very narrow sense in which the word 'coercion' is currently being used in British Military Doctrine. It is being limited specifically to 'strategic actions', that is those directed against governments and (in the context of civil war or insurgency) quasi-governmental leaderships. It is also being used purely for positive coercive strategic actions[8] in operations short of war – what are perhaps more properly called 'compellent' actions.

There are two fundamental problems for the crafters of military strategy and doctrine in this narrow focus. First is a legal problem. There is a widely held and defensible view that pre-emptive compellent actions are actually illegal unless mandated by the United Nations. Effective compellence[9] entails that force might actually be used in situations other than self-defence. As such they would be in breach of the United Nations Charter. The United States evades this legal problem by a broad interpretation of the concept of self-defence. Its air attacks against Libya in 1986 were a classic compellent action designed to halt state-sponsored terrorism by Libya. They were justified by the United States on the grounds of pre-emptive self defence, a concept that the United Kingdom does not accept.

The second problem is that the historical record for successful compellence is not good or is at best inconclusive. Indeed it is hard to find a historical example of successful compellence apart from the Libyan case. Even in this case there is no conclusive evidence that the Libyan government ceased to sponsor terrorism as a result of air attacks on Tripoli. Equally, it is not clear that air attacks brought the Bosnian Serbs to heel by compellence. The actions could equally be characterised as air interdiction on behalf of the Muslims and Croats which, coupled with outside reinforcement of these other parties, brought the Serbs to terms.[10] There are, on the other hand, some notable failures of compellence. Deployment of a task force to the South Atlantic in 1992 failed to persuade the Argentinean junta to withdraw forces from the Falklands. Similarly the deployment of coalition forces to the Gulf and the air campaign of the *Desert Shield* phase of the 1990-91 Gulf crisis failed to bring about a withdrawal of Iraqi forces from Kuwait. In both cases there was a resort to full combat.

The truth is that coercion must be understood in a wider context as an element of armed suasion[11] and that compellence is only one form of coercion. Maritime forces have a crucial role to play in armed suasion of which coercion is an important part but not the only part. It must be understood that posture as well as actions may influence the decision-making of governments and leaderships. Furthermore posture and actions that affect decision-making may not only be used to coerce. In many circumstances they might support or reassure, or communicate neutral signals of national, allied or coalition interest. This observation is particularly relevant to intervention in peace support or humanitarian operations where there may be several parties none of whom are opponents of the intervening forces *per se*.

As Cable, Luttwak, and other analysts of the diplomatic use of maritime power have emphasised, successful suasion will depend on creating the intended perception within the decision making process of the target leadership and that this is an inherently very risky business that could have unwanted consequences.

It is possible to relate the concepts of armed suasion, deterrence, coercion and compellence diagrammatically using a modification of Edward Luttwak's analysis from his book, *The Political Uses of Seapower*[12] (fig.1).

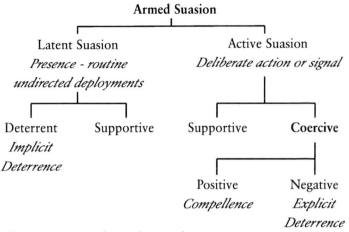

Figure 1: An Analysis of Ar med Suasion

From this analysis the relationship between deterrence and coercion becomes clear. There are two broad categories of deterrent action[13], explicit deterrence and implicit deterrence. One is coercive; the other is not strictly so. The advertisement of military capability and deterrent intentions to the world at large through deployment, exercising, declarations and policy statements is implicit deterrence if no particular target government or leadership is identified. It is a component of what in the maritime context is known as presence. Explicit deterrent actions are directed at an identified target government or leadership at a specific place and time, and are a negative form of coercion.

There are of course many degrees of coercive deployment from a veiled hint of a threat through full-scale demonstrations of force and acts of violence. At one end is what British maritime doctrine calls the 'symbolic' use where forces are 'used purely to signal a message to a specific government [or leadership] while not in themselves posing any threat to an opponent...'[14] Although symbolic use does not entail any actual threat, it must be distinguished from merely token use. The symbol is one of a greater force that could be used if necessary or indeed of other instruments of national power that could be deployed. There must be a clear association in the decision-making process of the target leadership between the symbol used and the greater power. This association depends on demonstrable capability and intention. Symbolic use cannot happen in isolation but must be supported by evidence of an expeditionary order of battle of which the symbol is an example, and a history of military engagement, of political resolve, and of exercises and demonstrations of military capability and readiness. Under these circumstances a frigate can be sufficient evidence of a nation that can project power in the form of carrier and amphibious task forces. Even a minehunter might be an adequate signal. However, a nation which has never exercised or used its forces in an expeditionary capacity or has never demonstrated political will to commit military force will find that its currency of symbols will have no value.

Symbolic use must be distinguished from other coercive uses in which the forces deployed to deter an aggressor or compel compliance could, indeed may actually, use violence in the course of their task. If sufficient, carefully tailored offensive force is deployed to creates the perception that it could hold at risk interests that a target leadership considers to be important. It gives evidence of the capability and will to use forces that might follow. One might coin the expression, 'explicitly coercive' for these uses.

One can distinguish a third type of coercive activity under the general category of armed suasion. British Maritime Doctrine refers to Preventive, Precautionary and Pre-emptive Naval Diplomacy for what Cable calls the 'catalytic' use of force. This important category is a peculiarly but not exclusively maritime phenomenon. There will be occasions particularly in the early stages of an emergent crisis when the specific policy objectives of a government or coalition in response to events are not clear. At best there may be broad objectives but these may not be sufficiently refined for positive military action; or they may be unprioritsed; or they may still be evolving.

Figure 2 is an idealised flow diagram of the process that governments need to follow in establishing a single grand strategic goal for military action in such a complex environment. It illustrates the problem of opaque policy objectives where, in Cable's words, the only option is to 'fish in muddy waters' (shown in grey). These situations are a land commander's worst nightmare and the military will usually counsel against involvement. However, naval forces can be very useful in these circumstances. For instance they can poise in theatre to avoid maldeployment and declare interest while they await more specific directives. They have the option of withdrawal if the situation becomes untenable. These circumstances are not unusual. They are a normal state of affairs in a troubled region. There may be real opportunities for preventive deployment, that is, one that contributes

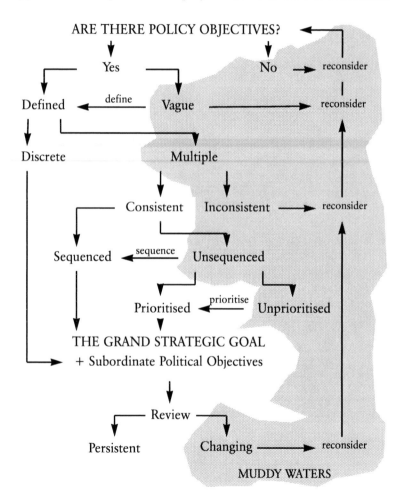

Figure 2:
The Process of Defining Policy Objectives - Idealised Flow Diagram

to prevents the crisis from developing. If military forces cannot operate in situations where a single discrete aim cannot be articulated, their usefulness for crisis prevention is severely limited. Maritime forces are well used to these situations.

Although naval forces have been historically associated with diplomatic use, coercive armed suasion is clearly not a role for maritime forces alone. Naval forces in particular, have some singular uses. Naval forces can create and exploit access from the sea. Their capacity to poise in theatre from the earliest stages of tension either overtly or covertly and with minimal diplomatic preparation is particularly useful to a government. They can maintain routine sustained presence in peacetime thereby contributing to a stable and peaceful environment. They can be deployed in the early stages of a developing crisis when commitment of ground and air forces is inappropriate or when the diplomatic environment does not permit suitable forward basing or overflying of foreign territory. They have particular uses when political objectives have not been refined beyond a general commitment to participation or action or when objectives are likely to change rapidly. They may be the only forces that can be deployed wisely when the risk of embroilment is high and where the sea provides the only avenue for coercive action.

There is , however, a penalty to flexibility and ease of withdrawal. Maritime forces do not signal as strong a commitment and political resolve as the insertion of ground forces. Similarly, the deployment of land based air forces can also signal a strong sense of common purpose with regional nations that have granted overflying and forward basing facilities. In a developed crisis it is likely that a range of joint capabilities will be used to coercive effect.

The arguments of this chapter can be summed up in the following propositions:

Successful coercive ar med suasion is about cor rect assessment of the values, objectives and perceptions of the tar get leadership. For this reason good political intelligence is a *sine qua non*. Some leaderships may be prepared to risk considerable damage to their infrastructure and death and injury to their populations. For example, even national survival may be sacrificed for transcendental aims such as those motivated by religion. Explicit coercion, whether deterrent or compellent, creates a perception of a threat to more or less clearly defined threats. They might be to: the personal security of the leadership; to the stabiliyt and survival of the regime; to higher command and control centres; to major armament and munitions concentrations; to key logistic nodes; or to key sites associated with national prestige (such as seaports, airports or local centres of government); to economies sensitive to blockade. These vulnerabilities must be correctly identified.

Early pre-emptive deterrent action is more likely to be effective than later compellent action. If action can be taken before a target leadership has established and agreed a plan, the coercion will be taken into consideration in the leadership's decision. More modest forces can be used for coercion at an early stage when symbolic action only may be required. Once a plan has been executed, it may be more difficult to halt or reverse by coercion. A climb-down or retreat may involve an unacceptable loss of face for an authoritarian regime. It is a common-sense maxim that deterrence is more likely to succeed than compellence.

It is easier to reinforce than to reverse a preferred course of action by coercion. This maxim is unprovable but intuitively sound. It is particularly relevant once a coercive operation is underway. If it is possible to create avenues or opportunities for metaphorical or physical retreat in the perceptions of the target leadership, it is more likely that the operation will be effective.

Use bold strokes. An incremental strategy is unlikely to be successful. Much is talked about menus of measured responses. Indeed the concept of a gradual increase in pressure is attractive to Western governments. However history shows that it is sudden increases or escalation of military activity or other forms of pressure that are more likely to influence the decisions of target leaderships. They and their populations will habituate to gradually increasing hardship and there may be a strengthening of resolve coupled with a sense of national alienation and common purpose. If coercing forces have the flexibility to escalate and can be reinforced easily, their effectiveness will be enhanced.

Coercion will be ineffective unless the forces involved have proven capabilities and their gover nments have a record of resolve. It may be necessary actually to use limited violence, even for a deterrent operation, to reinforce the message of capability and resolve. An unfortunate corollary is that regular use of force will have a positive cumulative effect on effective coercion.

Effective coercive suasion r elies on the perceived risk that failur e to comply will lead sooner or later to the commitment of over - whelming force. It is necessary to create and reinforce uncertainty as to how far the coercing government will go. It is insufficient merely to threaten to do a limited amount of damage and to create a cost benefit calculus in the minds of the target leadership. By the same token, coercing forces have their effect by their association with more substantial war-winning forces. A nation cannot procure limited capabilities specifically for coercive suasion.

Ar med suasion will invariably be conducted under close political control. It is a tool of government diplomacy in the most direct sense. One can forget elaborate layers of command structures based on rigid definitions of the levels of war. A lone frigate will be a strategic actor while it is engaged in a symbolic act of coercion.

There are a couple of themes that emerge from this discussion. First and foremost, armed suasion will be most effective if it is used as early as possible in an emerging crisis. It is at this stage that naval force can be uniquely useful. Secondly, when force is used for armed suasion, it is used in a military sense and not in some different way akin to policing or humanitarian use.[15] The forces that are employed are those that would be committed on a larger scale, if suasion failed and if full-scale extended combat were the only remaining option. Coercion is not merely some pre-combat function. It is the essence of combat itself.[16] Conversely combat capability is the essence of coercion. Gunboat diplomacy is not only for gunboats.

1   Coercion was, however, explored by theorists of the period particularly
    in the nuclear context, for example, Thomas C. Schelling in *Arms and
    Influence*, New Haven, Yale University Press, 1996.

2   *JWP 0-01: British Defence Doctrine,* London; Ministry of Defence,
    1997, pp 3.15 – 3.16.

3   *Gunboat Diplomacy 1919 - 1979,* Second Edition, London,
    Macmillan, 1981. There is a Third Edition , *Gunboat Diplomacy
    1919 - 1991,* London, Macmillan in association with IISS, 1994.

4   *Conventional Deterrence in the Changed Strategic Environment* (Final
    Version December 1993). This paper was cleared for publication in
    open source literature but never actually published. In consequence
    the charming sobriquet 'SOD' for a government or leadership that
    was a 'subject of deterrence' never saw the light of day. This chapter
    draws on some of the analysis in that paper.

5   Although a rather arcane expression, 'suasion' is not in fact a neologism
    (Chaucer, c1374) and has the advantage of being devoid of the
    nuances of some of the other expressions. Armed suasion was defined
    by Edward Luttwak in *The Political Uses of Seapower*, Baltimore MD,
    Johns Hopkins University Press, 1974, p. 10, as 'all reactions, political
    and tactical elicited by all parties – allies adversaries or neutrals – to
    the existence, display, manipulation, or symbolic use of any instrument
    of military power, whether or not such reactions reflect any deliberate
    intent of the deploying party. *BR 1806: The Fundamentals of British
    Maritime Doctrine,* London: HMSO, 1995, has a simpler definition
    that does not focus exclusively on the perceptions of the subject.
    The expression has not found its way into *British Defence Doctrine.*

6   Malcolm Rifkind's speech of 15 February 1994 on *Defence
    Capabilities.* In this speech Mr Rifkind referred to the utility of stand-
    off cruise missiles for the 'coercive use of force as an instrument of
    policy'.

7   See for example, Michael Clarke, 'Air Power and Force in Peace
    Support Operations', in Group Captain Andrew Lambert & Arthur
    C. Williamson eds., *The Dynamics of Air Power,* Bracknell UK, MOD,
    RAF Staff College, 1996.

8   *British Defence Doctrine* fails to make the distinction between
    coercion and its subset, compellence.

9   Luttwak *Op-Cit.* p. 5.

10 i.e. a situation in which further operations would have resulted in
    progressive loss of Serb held territory.

11 Luttwak does not restrict 'suasion' purely to the strategic level, i.e.
    influence upon governments. However Cable defines gunboat

diplomacy as a concept applying specifically to actions between governments. Where interstate conflict is not necessarily the norm, one must accept a broader definition that embraces other levels of war and that can applies to factions at the operational and even tactical level. It can be argued that a concept of suasion has application throughout the spectrum of conflict . However, it is situations short of open war and 'strategic actions' that that are under examination in this chapter.

12   Luttwak *Op-Cit.* Table 1. This modified version is drawn from the British Naval Staff paper, *Conventional Deterrence in the Changed Strategic Environment.*

13   There is actually a third category of deterrence, inherent or existential deterrence – the deterrent effect of the mere possession of a capability whether or not that capability is ever deployed. This form of deterrence is undirected as is implicit deterrence. It is therefore not strictly relevant to this discussion of coercion.

14   *BR1806,* pp. 89–90 and Glossary.

15   The author differs in view from other analysts who have identified a "Diplomatic" mode of using naval force. See K. Booth, *Navies and Foreign Policy,* London, Croom Helm, 1977; Eric Grove, *The Future of Seapower,* London, Routledge, 1990; and Geoffrey Till, *Maritime Strategy in the Nuclear Age,* (Second Edition), London, Macmillan, 1984.

Maritime Forces in Peace Support Operations

Michael Pugh

Maritime peace support operations are particularly important for influencing developments on land and there have been notable historical examples from which lessons can be drawn. To some extent the principles of maritime operations mirror those on land because of the peculiarities of international mandates, but maritime attributes also make distinctive contributions to international peace and security. In the context of an increasingly interdependent international system, peace support measures at sea are also important as a means by which national maritime forces develop multinational links.

There has not been a huge demand for traditional peacekeeping by maritime forces. As Douglas Johnston argues, there is rarely any urgency to resolve maritime issues, and policy differences do not become crises overnight because ocean territory issues lack symbolic and emotive content.[1] There are, of course, exceptions, particularly for coastal communities that depend on seaborne trade and marine resources for their livelihood and sustenance. But in general terms, disputes can be left simmering longer at sea because people do not live there.

Accordingly, there has been nothing comparable at sea to the interpositioning of blue beret troops between adversaries on land. In any case it would be risky for neutral ships to sustain that kind of stationary role. Visual and verbal communications for calming tense situations and avoiding accidental hostilities is more problematic, and the range of modern naval weapons poses a risk of disruptive over-the-horizon attacks. Maintaining an interposition between two or more manoeuvring naval forces is inherently difficult. To make an obvious point, blockades are only feasible because the landmasses being blockaded do not move!

But just because maritime operations cannot replicate all land-based operations does not make them any less important. They sustain and influence peace support operations on land, and some functions may be roughly comparable. In fact, during the League of Nations period, British and French naval vessels arrived off the coast of Flensburg, at Denmark's request, and sailors were landed as part of an international commission to police the plebiscite for Schleswig-Holstein in 1920. After the Second World War, the first UN observer mission (the UN Truce Supervision Organisation of 1948 or UNTSO, which kept a watch over the Palestine problem) was supported by an American aircraft carrier and three destroyers and a French minesweeper, flying a UN pennant below their national flags. The United States specified that its ships were only to engage in transport and observation functions (and the flagging can hardly be said to have set a precedent for the US Navy!)

MARITIME PEACE SUPPORT OPERATIONS

Nevertheless, since 1948 there have been several internationally authorised maritime components of peace support operations, including: in West New Guinea (1962-63); the Beira Patrol (1965-75); the Multinational Force and Observers in the Strait of Tiran (1982 to the present); operations to safeguard shipping in the Persian Gulf (1984-88); monitoring in the Gulf of Fonseca in Central America (1990-92); operations in the Adriatic (1991-96); operations in Cambodia (1992-94); and around Haiti (1992-94). Two of these, the Gulf of Fonseca and the Adriatic Sea operations, illustrate the contrasts between inoffensive peacekeeping and coercive sanctions monitoring/enforcement respectively.

The Gulf of Fonseca Patrols

These began on 29 June 1990 and ended on 17 January 1992, were commanded and controlled by the United Nations as part of the ONUCA (UN Central America Observers). With an eye to non-costly operational experience and enhancing its international respectability after the Falklands War, Argentina provided four 35-ton Israeli-built *Dabur* patrol craft from the Ushuaia base and 29 naval personnel. The boats patrolled the Gulf of Fonseca, river deltas and adjacent coastline, mainly to monitor any Nicaraguan gun-running to El Salvador. They flew the UN flag from the mainmast and the

Argentine flag from the stern and were painted white with UN lettering. in this respect it was a model peacekeeping operation of the classical, inoffensive type. The UN insisted that all weapons were removed and that crews were unarmed. Military Observers conducted observation tasks on board, but did not have the right to stop and inspect shipping and the squadron's ROE permitted only evasive action if threatened. The operation required nearly 6,500 patrol hours and was considered a useful contribution to the UN presence in deterring gun-running as part of a consent-based peace process.[2]

Adriatic operations

By contrast, the maritime peace support operations directed at the former Yugoslavia were not based on consent and in general the forces involved had a combat-ready configuration. Two naval groups, one NATO and the other WEU, were authorised to monitor the arms and trade embargoes. NATO units, stationed off Montenegro and the port of Kotor, and were commanded from Naples and comprised frigates or destroyers from Italy, the UK, Netherlands, Germany, Turkey, Greece and the United States. In January 1993 three carrier groups (US, UK and French) were also deployed with logistics experts, helicopters, escort vessels and auxiliaries. These ships assisted in the enforcement of a no-fly zone over Bosnia-Herzegovina. Additionally, the British and French ships offered contingency support, protection and a withdrawal capability for their UN troops ashore. A group co-ordinated by the WEU patrolled the Strait of Otranto, originally led by an Italian flagship and frigate. France, Belgium, Spain and Portugal each had a frigate, and there was a joint supply ship. The WEU also co-ordinated French, German, Italian and Dutch maritime air patrols based in Sicily. Initially the warships had no mandate to stop and search suspect vessels, but from 22 November 1992, in accord with UN Security Council Resolution 787, the Adriatic naval patrols were entitled to use necessary measures to enforce a blockade, even 'in the territorial sea of Serbia-Montenegro'. The ROE now allowed for firing across the bows of suspected vessels refusing to stop, though for political reasons German and Spanish warships were not engaged in enforcement activities. From 31 December 1992 Albania granted NATO unrestricted access to its territorial waters for purposes of embargo enforcement, and from 17 April 1993 the UN Security Council extended the mandate to prohibit all merchant ships from entering the territorial waters of Serbia-Montenegro except on a case-by-case basis or in the event of emergency. No ship was able to break the embargo after April 1993 and six were caught attempting to do so. The NATO/WEU groups were later combined into a single Task Force, although the carrier groups remained separate under national control. The operations were terminated on 1 October 1996 – after 74,192 merchants ships had been challenged, 5,951 had been boarded and inspected at sea and 1,480 diverted and inspected in port. This intensive effort by fourteen NATO/WEU members involved nearly 20,000 ship days at sea, over 7,000 maritime patrol aircraft sorties and over 6,000 AEW sorties.[3]

As these examples indicate, peace support tasks can range from monitoring and diplomatic presence to enforcement measures. The tasks which the RN recognises in its manual of doctrine *The Fundamentals of British Maritime Doctrine: BR 1806* are[4]:

- active monitoring of a sea area for infringement of sanctions/ embargo;

- patrolling and monitoring a maritime cease fire line or demilitarised zone;

- enforcement of sanctions/embargo;

- supervising cantonment of vessels;

- contribution of *organic* aircraft to enforcement of a *no fly zone* and *combat air support*;

- contribution of organic helicopters for in theatre movement of peacekeeping forces and humanitarian aid, and casualty evacuation;

- contribution of amphibious forces to ground peace support operations

- maintenance of an amphibious capability in theatre to permit withdrawal of peacekeeping forces aid workers and other civilians;

- provision of seaborne medical and other logistic and humanitarian resources where access by land is difficult;

- assistance to seaborne refugees;

- provision of a neutral platform for peace negotiations;

- mine countermeasures to provide access or contribute to a new peace.

Other categories of operation belong to the related concept of peacebuilding tasks (such as mine-clearing and rebuilding maritime infrastructures).

All the above tasks are marked out from other regular maritime activities by the political context from which key operational principles are derived. The basic principles of maritime peace support operations are similar to those devised for land operations.

- *Impartiality and neutrality* In peace support operations there is no enemy in a conventional sense. The UN, or other international organisation, attempts to act impartially between parties to the dispute and is neutral as to the outcome of a dispute. The political goals are to seek the consent of the parties to reach a political accommodation, to assist in recovery from conflict, to deter further conflict, to uphold international law and the legitimacy of the UN. The mandate usually reflects a political compromise and is often vague. But tailoring the operational instructions and ROE to the spirit of the mandate must be done with due regard to safety of vessels and crews and with great sensitivity to the political situation in the theatre of operations. Knowledge about the politics of the dispute and the importance of distinguishing, and if necessary protecting, non-combatants is important because peacekeepers have to stay on businesslike terms with all parties.

• *Inoffensive postures and conflict resolution techniques* One of the most important lessons drawn from the Gulf of Fonseca mission was the need for personnel to adapt from their preparation as warfighters to become inoffensive, highly visible and impartial sailors. The Nicaragua mission had more in common with a good-will visit to a friendly port than a military operation. It also means that naval personnel on UN operations have to acquire a particular outlook, an ethos, and particular skills. Peacekeepers often find that they need to achieve reassurance locally and to de-escalate potentially or manifestly violent situations. Peacekeepers need 'contact skills' involving communication and negotiation methods which help to create momentum towards resolution, or the facilitation of an atmosphere conducive to a pre-negotiated settlement.

• *Multinational co-operation* Peace support operations generally entail multinationalism and this requires an ability to work with nationalities that have different military cultures and *modus operandi.* Special arrangements for command and control, interoperability, allocation of tasks, communication links, ROE compatibility may have to be established.[5] Steps towards developing a common tactical doctrine also entails exercising with navies with varied cultures and procedures.

• *Special training* Obviously a great deal that naval personnel do will be familiar: in seamanship, navigation and communications. As Mats Berdal observes the special skills required for peacekeeping may be only 10% of the tasks.[6] But this 10% is significant because of the international political context. In rare situations where an 'enemy' is identified, international legitimacy has to be maintained, usually through the UN Security Council. Where a peace process is underway and strategic levels of consent are granted, the naval operations will have less in common with the kind of warfighting for which navies normally prepare.

The techniques, attributes and operational concepts applicable to peace support measures at sea are also bound to differ from those on land.

• *Accessibility, mobility and projection*: Ships are particularly well suited to diplomatic projection: showing the flag, monitoring situations, demonstrating involvement. They are also well suited to providing logistic support for land operations, amphibious and evacuation capabilities and offshore power in the event that force is used. This is partly because navies are subject to a distinctive legal regime. The high seas are beyond anyone's jurisdiction. Consent to innocent passage in territorial seas is not normally required, though there may be disputes about what constitutes innocent passage. Therefore the issue of consent does not arise in the same way as it does on land. Crossing into an EEZ or even a territorial sea does not have the same political impact as troops crossing a land frontier.

• *Versatility*: Ships can provide a great range of options. Unless small craft of opportunity are used, the UN has to rely on warships. When a warship puts to sea, whether it is going on a drug interdiction mission, a warfighting mission or a peacekeeping mission it will generally turn out with the capability to defend itself. It may set out with a pacific intention, but its appearance and capability gives it a warfighting face. This can create problems in signalling intent, but can also have advantages in situations which may escalate (as in the Adriatic after 22 November 1992), and in creating ambiguity for purposes of deterrence.

• *Endurance*: Given that the goal of such operations is not victory in battle, and since non-military settlements can take a long time to reach or be implemented, long-term patrolling for observation or monitoring is to be expected. Ships are particularly suited to this as demonstrated by the two examples above.

• *Response*: Ships are useful for peacekeeping because they can be assembled and sent to distant areas in a relatively short time scale.

• *Symbolism*: Ships are political symbols which convey political messages. They are thus particularly useful at signalling UN interest in a problem or demonstrating concern.

The future of peace support operations at sea depends ultimately on the evolution of international politics. It is sometimes argued that there are inherent operational and technical obstacles to the international integration of maritime forces. However, if political relations between states are good, then operational integration can follow. NATO's experience indicates that training, doctrine, intelligence and technical issues can be addressed successfully when political consensus is present.

In the heyday of Mahan's influence in the nineteenth and early twentieth centuries, maritime power was regarded as a kind of virility symbol of nationhood. The concept of navies as instruments of state competition traditionally took precedence over ideas of international co-operation. Maritime power was associated with prestige, empire, preparation for war against defined enemies and gunboat diplomacy.[7] However, four countervailing factors are likely to map out a different kind of post-cold war future for maritime forces at least in the seas in which the Royal Navy will concentrate its peace and security roles.

First, processes of globalization have diminished the effects of national sovereignty and national power. To cite just one manifestation, it has become increasingly difficult to find a rationale for national protection of national merchant shipping. It is perhaps a pardonable exaggeration to say that the states with the largest shipping registers have no navies and the states with the largest navies have no shipping registers. There are no great Liberian, Panamanian or Maltese navies and, as in the 'Tanker War' in the Persian Gulf, the larger navies end up protecting merchant ships registered under flags of convenience.

Second, the internationalisation of the legitimate use of power shows little sign of diminishing in spite of the setbacks experienced by the United Nations, EU and CSCE in the Balkans and elsewhere. The authorisation of force by the UN as a universally-recognised legitimating body is seen as a potentially useful instrument in US foreign policy.[8] Moreover, the demand for multinational peace support operations is unlikely to evaporate. Humanitarian crises are an abiding feature of a system in which the gap between rich and poor states is widening, and in which the authority of some central governments collapses or communities seek greater autonomy. The main change from the early 1990s will be that potential interventionists will be more selective about when and where they get involved.

Third, the process of regime formation is likely to continue. Of course, seafarers have long had a common interest in developing rules and regulations for conduct at sea (such as the Collision Prevention Regulations). Together with the UN Law of the Sea Convention these amount to a functional international maritime regime to promote peacetime norms of behaviour at sea, overseen by the UN's International Maritime Organisation. Spillover into security relations is also evident, and not merely between alliance members. Contacts between the personnel of different security cultures have fostered mutual confidence - even when general political conditions are unfavourable - as demonstrated by the Incidents at Sea Agreements of the Cold War period. Furthermore, peace support operations since the Gulf War have fostered links between maritime forces and these could become increasingly institutionalised.

Fourth, the process of integration through division of labour and burden-sharing within collective security arrangements is likely to continue, albeit at a slow pace, because of its perceived cost benefits. These processes are intensified either in circumstances of common perceptions of an imminent threat or when resource constraints make it very difficult for national forces to maintain all-round, autonomous capabilities. A west European navy may be as far off as a UN navy, but at the very least, if the resource squeeze currently affecting Western navies continues, then we can expect further co-operation on the lines of EURMARFOR and the joint Dutch-Belgian naval command announced in 1995.[9]

CONCLUSION

Given that the UN is unlikely to acquire its own navy, large-scale operations, especially enforcement operations, will probably have to be franchised to `coalitions of the willing and able'. Organisations such as NATO have a comparative advantage in the provision of enforcement. Reliance on the capabilities of such core coalitions may be necessary to give peace support operations credibility. However, credibility has to be balanced against legitimacy.[10] Problems can flow from naval operations that are perceived as a form of gunboat diplomacy conducted by the rich and powerful states for naked national interests at the expense of poorer states. Legitimacy in the use of force for purposes of international peace and security, as well as the legitimacy of the UN itself, ultimately depends on perceptions of political acceptability. In this respect it is perhaps as essential for policy makers to facilitate an inclusive, rather than exclusive, view of contributions to maritime peace support measures and to assist in building up the expertise of smaller maritime powers accordingly.

1. Douglas M. Johnston. (1988). *The Theory and History of Ocean Boundary-Making.* Kingston, Ontario, McGill-Queen's University Press.

2. Juan Carlos Neves. (1993). *United Nations Peace-Keeping Operations in the Gulf of Fonseca by Argentine Navy Units.* Report 01-93, Strategy and Campaigns Dept., US Naval War College, Newport RI. January 1993.

3. NATO/WEU Operation Sharp Guard, IFOR Final Factsheet. 2 October 1996. Available on-line: <http://www.nato.int/ifor/ifor.htm>.

4. *The Fundamentals of British Maritime Doctrine: BR 1806.* Directorate of Naval Staff Duties (DNSD), Royal Navy. D/DNSD 8/36. London, Her Majesty's Stationery Office. 1995. p.93.

5. In the Haiti operation of 1993–94 a Multinational Force was under US command but there were six national ROE (see: Commander Peter Jones Royal Australian Navy. `Multinational Operations: Their Demands and Impact on Medium Power Navies.' Paper presented at Conference on: Medium Power Navies; Challenges, Roles and Issues in an Era of Collective Security. University of British Columbia, 23-25 February 1995.

6. Mats Berdal. (1993). *Whither UN Peacekeeping?* Adelphi Paper, no.281. London, International Institute for Strategic Studies (IISS). October 1993.

7. See Michael Pugh, 'Is Mahan Still Alive? State Naval Power in the International System', in *Journal of Conflict Studies*, vol.16, no.2. Fall 1996. pp.109–24.

8. See Phyllis Bennis, (1996). *Calling the Shots: How Washington Dominates Today's UN.* New York, Olive Branch Press; Michael MacKinnon, *Fairweather Friend? Policy for UN Peace Support Operations Policy under the Clinton Administration.* London, Frank Cass (forthcoming, 1997).

9. See generally, Geoffrey Till, 'Europe's Maritime Strategy: Present Context and Future Directions', in Gert de Nooy, (ed.), (1996). *The Role of European Naval Forces after the Cold War.* The Hague, Netherlands Institute of International Relations and Kluwer Law International. p.35.

10. See Michael Pugh, *From Mission Cringe to Mission Creep? Some Implications of Peace Support Operations Doctrine.* Oslo, Norwegian Institute for Defence Studies. Forthcoming.

The Royal Navy in the Last Long Peace: 1815-1914

Andrew Lambert

At the end of the Napoleonic wars Britain emerged, her territorial ambitions fully satisfied, as a unique and truly global power. British statesmen had exploited the peace treaties of 1814-15 to establish a stable and balanced European order, and to retain the key strategic naval bases of Malta, the Ionian Islands, the Cape of Good Hope, Ceylon and Mauritius. These new bases enabled the Navy to protect British trade and interests outside Europe while, at the same time, providing the defence of the home islands. The Navy was paid for by a strong economy, based on a powerful combination of trade, industry and financial services. On the negative side of the equation Britain had built up a massive level of national debt during the twenty one year war with France, and for much of the next half century servicing this debt severely constrained defence expenditure. The post war reconstruction of the Navy was a relatively slow process, dominated by the establishment of the 'Two-Power Standard' in 1817. The Navy was to be equal to the combined strength of the next two largest fleets, which were then, and would remain until 1905, those of France and Russia. Only through the possession of overwhelming naval power could Britain retain her diplomatic freedom, avoiding the need to enter European alliance systems in peacetime.

It should be stressed that Britain had no ambitions that required her to go to war, only interests and possessions that might have to be defended. Therefore British strategy throughout the long peace was deterrent. Avoiding war through the possession of overwhelming strength at sea was a far cheaper method of defending a global empire than any system of fixed fortifications and military garrisons. The same fleet could deter all major powers, and the land frontiers of India were, it was realised after the disasters of the First Afghan War, (1839-1843) more easily secured against Russia by sending a fleet to St. Petersburg than an army to Kabul. Throughout the long peace Britain used her naval power to deter powerful rivals from threatening her interests, avoiding the need to fight. Deterrent strategies will only work when they are based on a credible threat that is clearly understood by the power to be deterred, and effectively signalled, usually through a large scale mobilisation, linked to political action. This strategy had been developed over time, England, and later Britain, had used deterrent strategies in the sixteenth, seventeenth and eighteenth centuries. In the nineteenth century it became the core British policy.

British deterrence was based on a war fighting strategy that reflected the experience of the preceding twenty one years. It would be enhanced by the application of new technologies to the role of naval forces. The Napoleonic wars had demonstrated that, although naval power could not overthrow a major European state, it could preserve Britain, her empire and her trade, while inflicting massive, cumulative economic attrition on any state, including the Napoleonic European super-state and the supposedly 'self-sufficient' Russian Empire, which was crippled by preventing the export of primary produce. The key to this strategy was the maintenance of command of the sea, the ability to use the sea for strategic and commercial purposes, while denying it to others. The command of the sea, allied to financial, economic and industrial strength, would allow Britain to wage long wars of limited military commitment in which economic attrition would eventually wear down even the most powerful military states.

After Trafalgar the Royal Navy had re-invented itself as a power projection force, building up an impressive track record in amphibious and coastal operations, the largest of which were designed to destroy the naval power of the enemy. The capture of Copenhagen in 1807 was the best example, it resulted in the capture of the entire Danish Navy, and almost everything of value in Copenhagen dockyard. It was this operation which Lord Fisher threatened to repeat at Wilhemshaven in 1907. Operations of this type, launched at the outbreak of war, would secure command of the sea, and demonstrate to hostile powers the utter futility of making war on Britain.

The application of steam, rifled guns, armour plate and other technologies merely enhanced and furthered the deterrent power of the Royal Navy. Steam allowed large ships to operate close to the land, and in major rivers, it enabled ships to outflank old systems of coastal defence based on the threat of sailing ships, and vastly increased the range and sustainability of amphibious operations. When allied with armour and heavy guns, steam gave a dominant navy, like the Royal Navy, or the Federal Navy in the American Civil War, the capacity to attack and destroy large coastal fortifications, and carry naval strength into the heart of a rival naval base. It was to counter this threat that weaker naval powers developed modern defensive systems; mines, torpedoes and submarines. These, in turn, prompted new counter-measures; the Royal Navy first carried out large scale minesweeping off Cronstadt in 1855.

The development of this dynamic offensive element in naval planning was intimately linked to the growth of the French base at Cherbourg. The completion of a vast enclosed basin, and the construction of a rail link to Paris, gave France the facilities to threaten a cross-channel invasion. However, the Royal Navy responded by building new bases at Portland, Dover and Alderney, from which to conduct a steam blockade of Cherbourg, and in which to collect steam powered assault shipping to demolish the dockyard and burn the shipping. The 'Cherbourg' Strategy required flotilla craft for long range bombardment with guns, rockets and mortar vessels. They would be supported by steam powered assault ships, initially old battleships, but later specialist armoured shallow draft types euphemistically referred to as 'coast defence ships', which would rely on their weight of fire and protection to enable them to operate at close range. The various specialist warships would be used in a layered attack, with the defences being suppressed by long range fire, the dockyard bombarded, and then, if the opportunity arose the assault craft breaking into the harbour to complete the task. The main battlefleet would not be used for these dangerous and costly operations, the command of the sea was too important to risk in an engagement with masonry and earthworks. That did not mean that naval forces would not act offensively, merely that the right types of craft had to be procured to provide the fleet with the full range of capabilities.

Between 1815 and 1914 the Royal Navy used this deterrent strategy, combining the economic and strategic power for a long war with the dynamic offensive element to cripple rival navies at the outset, to deter all four of the major powers of the age from attacking vital British interests. The finest testimony to the power and strength of the Royal Navy in the nineteenth century came in the very solid form of massive fortifications surrounding the naval bases and coastal cities of Britain's rivals. In December 1861 the threat to her eastern seaboard persuaded the American Government to give way, in 1878 and 1885 mobilising an assault fleet at Spithead to attack Cronstadt led Russia to pull back from Istanbul and then Afghanistan, in 1898 the threat to demolish Cherbourg led France to give way in the Fashoda Crisis, and seven years later the sudden appearance of the British fleet in the Baltic persuaded Imperial Germany not to push France too far over Morocco. In all cases Britain's best interests were served by the preservation of the *status quo*.

The same equipment that was needed to carry out coastal offensive operations against first class naval bases was, by no coincidence, ideally suited to small scale littoral warfare against less powerful states. As a result the gunboat, designed to attack Cherbourg, and built to bombard Cronstadt, was used to defeat China in the late 1850s, and became the symbol of Imperial power across the globe.

However, while British strategy was unique, and largely successful, it was neither cheap nor infallible. In order to secure command of the sea, based on a two power standard the Royal Navy was forced to keep abreast of all the technical developments of the nineteenth century, and keep a large fleet of the most modern and powerful ships. As Britain was uniquely vulnerable to a superior navy the construction of a powerful fleet by any of her rivals was a direct challenge to her diplomatic independence long before it was a threat to her insular security. France, and later Imperial Germany, would build large and very expensive battlefleets in this period, attempting to coerce Britain into supporting their ambitions in Europe and the wider world. Under Louis Napoleon III (1852-1870) France built a wooden steam battlefleet and then an ironclad battlefleet in an effort to secure British support for a general reconstruction of the European state system. Successive British governments responded by engaging the French in an arms race, relying on the technical, industrial and financial superiority of the British state, symbolised by the pioneer ironclad HMS *Warrior* of 1861. By 1865 France had conceded defeat.

In 1898 Kaiser Wilhelm II and Admiral Tirpitz launched a programme to build a battlefleet with the express intention of securing British neutrality in the event of a major European war. Once again a naval race was begun, by Admiral Sir John, later Lord, Fisher with the epochal battleship HMS *Dreadnought* in 1906, which Germany could not afford to win. By 1912 Germany had recognised her defeat, and by 1914 Anglo-German relations were much improved. In the interval Britain had aligned, but not allied, herself with France and Russia, in order to preserve the balance of power in Europe, a balance *temporarily* upset by the disastrous Russian war with Japan. By 1914 the balance was essentially restored, and Britain was anxious not to give France and Russia any encouragement to start a war.

Unfortunately the deterrent strategy did not work on all occasions. It relied on the leaders of hostile states acting rationally, and had to be clearly and effectively signalled. In 1853 the British government did not attempt to deter Russia, for a variety of reasons connected with a fractured coalition government, a fragile relationship with France and a general reluctance to rely on force. As a result the Russians were allowed to think that Britain was not serious until they had committed themselves to far to pull back. The result was the Crimean War, which took over two years to resolve, at great coast in life and treasure. On the positive side the war did demonstrate the range and power of Britain's maritime strategy, and ended with a great fleet review at Spithead on St. George's Day 1856, when the fully mobilised offensive power of the Royal Navy was given a very public demonstration, before the massed civil and military representatives of all the major powers of the world.

More seriously the British Government made no effort to use naval power as a deterrent in July 1914. Because they did not understand how British strategy functioned the ministers, greatly distracted by other issues, and unwilling to believe that Germany meant to start a war, did not issue a warning to Germany until she crossed the Belgian frontier. By this time it was too late. More seriously the symbol of British power and commitment, the battlefleet, which had already been mobilised, was not used to signal British concern. Having adopted a war-fighting strategy of 'distant blockade', and concerned that the Germans might launch a surprise attack at, or even before, the outbreak of war, the First Lord of the Admiralty hastily removed the Grand Fleet from Portland and hid it at Scapa Flow. As a result neither Britain, nor the powerful naval force she had built to preserve her international position had any influence on the events leading to the outbreak of the First World War. This was not because Britain, or seapower, were irrelevant, merely a severe lesson in the vital necessity for a coherent, professional approach to the formulation and conduct of state policy. In 1854 and 1914 the outbreak of war might not have been avoidable, but on both occasions the ministers concerned were at fault for not trying. In 1914 the results of their negligence would be disastrous.

The Royal Navy was the core of British strategy between 1815 and 1914, it secured a unique global empire, deterred major powers from threatening Britain, or the interests she considered vital, and did so at very low real cost. National strategy was maritime. It had been built on the experience of the French Wars, enhanced by the application of new technology and applied by statesmen and naval officers of vision, like Lord Palmerston and Lord Fisher, to avoid costly and counter-productive wars. In consequence Britain secured the 'Lion's share' of the globe and its trade, while avoiding major wars. This was the result of her unique strategic posture, and the overwhelming naval strength upon which it was based. It is only through the intelligent formulation of long term policies that build upon historical experience, and co-ordinate foreign relations, national strategy and naval policy into a unified whole that the best interests of the nation can be served without excessive expenditure on defence. The nineteenth century provides a impressive demonstration of how this process can be conducted.

The Royal Navy - The View From a Distance

James Goldrick

The Royal Navy approaches the millennium with a mixture of confidence in its capabilities and recent achievements and uncertainty for the future. Both confidence and uncertainty are justified. It may be an exaggeration to state the Royal Navy is at a crossroads, but it is certainly clear that the strategic and force structure decisions made in the next few years will determine whether the navy diminishes by slow degrees into a purely northern European force or continues to be a major element in the ability of the Western Alliance to project power over long distances.

In force structure terms, the Royal Navy has managed the change from a Cold War posture relatively well. Indeed, the obvious ease with which the operational fleet made the transition to the requirements of a complex "New World Order" are something of a tribute to the tenacity with which successive naval staffs maintained the holy grail of a balanced fleet against the claims of those who gave primacy to the Soviet threat alone. Perhaps the lessons of the Falklands campaign were instrumental in allowing the balance to be sustained in the last years of the Cold War, but in any event the operational tempo of the last seven years is its own indication of the flexibility and utility of naval forces.

The major casualties of the reduction process were the diesel submarines and a good proportion of the nuclear submarine fleet. What remains, however, is still one of the most capable underwater forces in the world and, with twelve attack type submarines (SSNs) in service and at least three new generation units on the way, fully capable of meeting any likely requirement. The most modern SSNs are being fitted with *Tomahawk* cruise missiles, the first step in a process which may see many more carried elsewhere in the fleet. In the final stages of completion, the quartet of *Trident* boats will place relatively modest demands on the naval budget in the future and suggestions that strategic deterrence is in some way not a truly naval role are now rarely heard. Whether the four submarines remain purely nuclear weapons platforms is, however, somewhat less clear. The United Kingdom will obviously retain the nuclear capability indefinitely, but the possibilities for extending the use of the ships into precise conventional strike missions, perhaps with *Tomahawk* missiles, must be very attractive for the long term.

Key to the attempts to maintain a fleet capable of distant operations and the projection of power ashore have been retention of the three *Invincible* class carriers, construction of the helicopter assault ship *Ocean* and the order for the assault ships *Albion* and *Bulwark*. The latter will complete much later than the Royal Navy would like, faced as it is with the prospect of running on the near moribund *Intrepid* and *Fearless* in the interim, but the total capability is well balanced and adequate. For their part, the Royal Marines have reached an "irreducible minimum" and a balance between front line and support forces which, however light their scale of equipment in land warfare terms and however great their reliance upon indirect support from both RN and British Army, is extremely impressive.

The air groups carried within the *Invincibles* have proved capable and flexible, particularly with the type mixing that is possible when the Royal Air Force GR7 *Harriers* are added to the *Sea Harriers*. This has proved a very effective combination to meet the demands of strike and air defence and is likely to see use well into the future. Future fighter and Aerial Early Warning capabilities are not yet an issue, but staff considerations in these areas and for some kind of follow on for the *Invincibles* are likely to consume increasing time and energy over the next decade. However innovative the final solution, deployable air power on at least the same scale will be vital to maintaining current power projection capabilities.

The Fleet Train remains a notable force multiplier for the Royal Navy. The lessons of the 1945 Pacific campaign, in which the British fleet struggled to operate with makeshift and inadequate logistic support, were learned well. The RN's sustainment capabilities are second only to those of the much larger USN and add considerable credibility to the navy's claims of strategic reach. If the carriers are one vital British contribution to European naval capabilities, then the replenishment force is certainly another.

There have been reductions elsewhere, particularly in the frigate and destroyer force, but these were foreshadowed as long ago as 1984 when it became clear that the Conservative government then in power was not maintaining a building programme sufficient to maintain a 50 ship force, the officially stated minimum level. The current strength of approximately 36 units is a result of that approach and was foreseen at the time by outside observers. The difficulty for the RN is not in the age or condition of the majority of these ships, particularly as the Type 23s continue to emerge from the builders' yards, but in the design bias of the newer units, including the later Type 22s, towards anti-submarine warfare (ASW) and anti-nuclear submarine warfare at that. These ships certainly have considerable general purpose capabilities in the form of guns, helicopters, surface to surface missiles and (particularly) excellent electronic warfare systems, however they lack area anti-air warfare (AAW) defence capabilities. These are currently provided by the Type 42 destroyers with their *Sea Dart* missiles but both ships and their systems are ageing and modernisation is in no way an attractive option. The erstwhile replacement, the European Common New Generation Frigate (CNGF) frigate is not only suffering from the apparently inevitable delays associated with multi-national projects but has very serious questions over the level of AAW capability which the intended radars and missiles will confer in the twenty first century. There can be no doubt, even if ASW assumes new importance with the proliferation of conventional submarines in smaller navies, that AAW remains the key for the survival of surface forces and in the support such ships can give to land forces in high technology conflicts. The Royal Navy is certainly willing, as its attempts to involve itself in the American efforts at Co-operative Engagement Capability (CEC) and Theatre Ballistic Missile defence indicate, but the force structure spirit is weak and will remain so until a capability broadly equivalent to the American *Aegis* system goes to sea. The problem is that the process of achieving that capability will be very expensive indeed and will probably force further reductions amongst the frigates to provide the necessary resources.

On a smaller scale, but hardly less significant, are the mine countermeasure forces of the Royal Navy. These, too, are experiencing considerable pressure, even though an order for an additional seven

Sandown class minehunters was finally placed in 1994. The navy is doing what it can to maintain force levels and some of the older *Hunt* class minehunters are being dual-roled as Northern Ireland patrol vessels to keep them in service. Retention of a strong and highly credible MCM force will, however, not only be important for the defence of the United Kingdom itself, but as a contribution to coalition efforts which cannot fully be matched by any other European power or even, arguably, by the United States. Similar arguments apply to the retention as a military service of the Hydrography Branch, albeit much more commonly in the form of naval parties on chartered vessels than in commissioned HM Ships. Less well protected, however, are lower level tasks such as fisheries. The Fishery Protection Squadron, despite its history as one of the oldest formed RN squadrons, may be at risk of replacement by commercial or non-military government operations. The whole question or whether or not there should be some form of all embracing national sea safety and environmental management agency must be as much an issue in Britain as it is in other maritime states.

In an intellectual sense, the Royal Navy faces three challenges. The first will be to ensure national understanding of its roles and its essential utility in war and peace. The second will be to sustain an adequate internal understanding of the navy's place in British society, its functions and its future. The third, in a general way already achieved and requiring a "continuing on of the same", will be to enforce upon the outside world recognition of its professionalism and capabilities. The first two requirements are inter-related and will be highly complex in their realisation. The RN is coming to terms with the fact that it is not a big navy. There no longer exist the mechanisms within the Service sufficient to provide answers for every problem. The commercialisation of much activity following *Front Line First* and other attempts at reducing the defence infrastructure are one, sometimes misdirected aspect of this reality. So is the increasing drive towards joint structures, a process in which the Royal Navy has found itself not always at ease with the Army's tendency to assume that "joint means green". So too will be the willingness to avoid the "not invented here" syndrome and make use of the best, and most affordable of foreign inventions and equipment. This is something at which the Royal Navy has tended to be rather better than British industry but there will remain pressures to support local manufacturers which may not be in the best interests of restricted budgets and all round fighting capabilities.

That there are uncertainties over the relationship between the navy and the nation have been manifest in the debates over women at sea and homosexuals within the Armed Forces. The lack of coherency in much that was said was indicative of the problem. The difficulty was not that the Navy, or the other services, believed that they differed from ordinary society in their expectations and requirements, but that there was a degree of uncertainty in the declaration of those differences and the arguments which were deployed. The controversial series on HMS *Brilliant* was not well received within the Royal Navy, but the truth is that the picture, albeit slanted, was one recognised by those who had served with but not in the RN as being reasonably accurate. In other words, the RN has not yet wholly succeeded in reconciling its historically derived self image with the wholly, indeed extraordinarily professional but rather more mundane contemporary reality.

There is certain to be pressure on the Royal Navy if any further reductions are forced on the defence budget as a whole. Given the emerging strategic policies of a Labour government very much set upon maintaining British engagement in a world wide context - and the healthy state of the economy - there is no immediate reason why such reductions should be a priority. The issue, however, remains one of justifying resources against what seem to many to be uncertain returns. In this, there is a fundamental problem of educating the national consciousness which the Royal Navy has never faced before.

Professor Paul Kennedy remarked in his recent Roskill lecture at Cambridge of the extent to which engagement of the British population in the maritime world as a whole has diminished and suggested that this must have profound implications for the naval case in the future. This is undeniable. The form, substance and intended audience for any "naval case" must adjust to the changing environment, particularly when the extent of previous military experience within Parliament and the other arms of government is diminishing rapidly.

The great mass of British trade remains seaborne, despite the completion of the Channel Tunnel, but it flows to and from northern Europe by routes on which the passage time is calculated in hours rather than days. Britain's commercial interests further afield, while vast, are more often in investment rather than direct trade. The reasons for hard commitments elsewhere seem, on the face if it, to have diminished considerably in recent years. The transfer of Hong Kong to China marked an effective end of Empire for Britain in the Asia-Pacific region. Britain's place, if there is one in security issues far afield from northern Europe, will thus have to be determined by the degree to which its interests can be served by military presence and military commitment. That judgement must be justified clearly and comprehensively to the public at large.

Once that judgement is made, and there are obvious and extremely valuable contributions which British maritime forces can offer to security arrangements in several key regions, the need will be for proofs of such a commitment by means of frequent deployments and active exercise programmes. Furthermore, while there is a natural tendency to take advantage of well publicised visits by ships to foreign ports to promote British trade as a whole, it will be important for the Royal Navy to hold its national defence industry at arms length if its ships are not to be seen simply as demonstrator models, brought to a particular area to allow would-be customers a close up look.

As with other navies, and perhaps more than some, the Royal Navy faces great challenges in retaining its experienced personnel, most notably in the technical specialisations. The interest expressed by many officers and ratings in the recent redundancy programme indicated that there was no reason for complacency, despite good pay and continuing efforts to improve conditions of service. The pressure and pace of contemporary naval operations are such that there is a risk of "burn out" if personnel are not allocated a reasonable measure of shore time. The danger with *Front Line First* and similar exercises is that the uniformed support infrastructure will be reduced to a point such that there is no possibility of allowing a workable ratio of sea to shore time. Furthermore, retention must also depend upon the degree of confidence which personnel have in the nation's commitment to the navy.

Relations with the other services remain an important issue. While the RAF has its own questions to resolve over the shape and size of the air force and its role in the emerging defence strategy, the most delicate problem is interaction and the degree of integration necessary with the British Army. The Falklands aside, the latter has not been comprehensively engaged in a maritime or expeditionary, as opposed to continental environment for many years. The experience of Bosnia may have gone a little way towards demonstrating something of what maritime forces are and are not capable, but there will be much more to do in terms of joint education over the next few years.

In all, the Royal Navy can face the future with no complacency but a substantial degree of hope. Its record of achievement and readiness to perform must appeal to a young and energetic government with realistic ideas as to Britain's limitations but a shrewd understanding of its very significant capabilities. In its operations, the RN will never again "always travel first class", but it possesses sufficient technology and more than sufficient expertise in operating that technology to ensure that its accomplishments will always be of the highest order.

Natural and Necessary Allies:
The Anglo-American Partnership at Sea*

Jan S. Breemer

"Let each nation (England and America) be educated to realize the length and breadth of its own interest in the sea; when that is done the identity of those interests will become apparent." *Alfred Thayer Mahan*

Introduction

In a speech before a gathering of international naval officers in November 1995 Admiral Jeremy Boorda, then the US Navy's Chief of Naval Operations (CNO), spoke of the importance to his navy of an international "partnership from the sea."[1] Partnerships between navies and naval officers, he said, be it by way of formal alliances or less formal relationships, are at the "foundation of our common future security" – in war and in peace.[2] The CNO offered a number of reasons why the US Navy, though the largest and most powerful navy in the world by far, yet needs dependable naval allies to deter conflict and, if need be, exercise force. His basic message: coalition partners contribute capabilities and expertise the US Navy does not own and cannot afford.

Few observers of the international naval scene doubt that the Royal Navy occupies a special place among the US Navy's collaborative navy–to–navy relationships. This paper is about this relationship, its origins, and why Anglo-American collaboration at sea remains a natural and necessary partnership for global stability and security.

A Special Relationship

The Anglo-American naval partnership is arguably at the heart of the "special relationship" that has long distinguished the Anglo-American security connection. This special relationship is commonly traced back to World War II, or as some historians have it, the Cold War era. According to the latter, the need in Britain for a special relationship with the United States arose from an awareness of the country's diminished strength in the post-World War II world. When he returned from his talks with President Truman and other high-level American officials in December 1950, Prime Minister Attlee proudly informed his cabinet colleagues that Britain had been "lifted of the 'European queue' and treated as the United States's 'principal ally.'"3 The phrase "special relationship" may be the invention of the Cold War, but as this paper proposes, its substance goes as far back as the 1820s.

The roots of the unique transatlantic security linkage lie, first an foremost, in the most basic of shared experiences, i.e. a common heritage, political culture, and, of course, language. But while this has been a necessary condition, it has never been sufficient. The *substance* of the Anglo-American security connection, notably its naval dimension, has hinged on what has long been a shared perspective on global stability and security. Again, the origins of this shared perspective are much older than the World War II, the Cold War, or even World War I. To be sure, the emergence of a common military threat in each of these episodes strengthened the Anglo-American partnership and gave it a special immediacy, but the basis was laid as far back as the formative years of the Monroe Doctrine early in the last century. More on those formative years is said later on. Let it suffice at this point to note its longevity: the common Anglo-American understanding of the conditions for global peace and security has outlasted more than a century of vast geo-political changes - from the collapse of the Spanish empire in the Americas and Far East, through the rise and fall of the Second and Third *Reichs*, and to, most recently, the downfall of the Soviet empire. One is tempted to conclude that the Anglo-American security connection has, over the years, become a tradition, perhaps even an international *norm*. Throughout, the partnership of the US and Royal navies has commonly been the instrument-of-choice for giving substance and effect to this norm.

The Roots of A Tradition

The Anglo-American naval link goes back to the early part of the last century. It was in the early 1820s that British Forein Minister George Canning proposed an Anglo-American alliance to safeguard the independence of the New World against Europe's Quadruple Alliance. Former US Presidents Jefferson and Madison advised acceptance of the British offer, for as Madison put it, "with the British power and navy combined with our own, we have nothing to fear from the rest of the world."[4] President Monroe and his Secretary of State, John Quincy Adams disagreed, chosing instead to issue a unilateral declaration which became known as the Monroe Doctrine. The Americans knew, as did the British, that the young republic had no capacity to speak of to enforce the declaration; for all intents and purposes, and until well into the century, keeping Europe's major continental powers out of the Americas depended on Pax Britannica, backed by the guns of the Royal Navy.

Through most of the nineteenth century, the United States was preoccupied with the consolidation of a continental empire; few of its citizens thought of their country as a maritime nation whose safety and prosperity hinged on a fleet capable of enforcing security at sea. The conclusion of the American Civil War and subsequent period of Reconstruction signaled the completion of the process of continental maturation, and American industry and agriculture in the 1870s produced surpluses that needed overseas outlets. It also happened to be the decade which, it is commonly agreed, saw the beginning of the end of the century's international economic order based on the principles of free trade, non-discrimination, and equal treatment. Nations on both sides of the Atlantic resurrected the older mercantile strategies - raising tariffs on foreign imports and, most important, scrambling to acquire secure – and monopolistic – access to overseas markets and sources of raw materials. It required little imagination for attentive Americans to make the connection between national growth and a navy sufficient to protect the country's overseas trade. As one Congressman put it: "Our future growth lies in the success of our commerce, and no great commerce has ever been built up without the assistance of a navy to protect the merchant marine and enforce the rights of merchants and traders."[5]

The upshot was the creation, beginning in the late 1880s, of America's "New Navy." It received its firey baptism just before the close of the century at Santiago and Manila Bays. Britain alone among the European Great Powers supported the US intervention.

"Official opinion" in Britain, reported US Ambassador John Hay from London, urged that the United States "take Cuba at once." Even more, he continued, "If we wanted it – which, of course, we do not – we could have the practical assistance of the British navy – on the *do ut des* principle, of course."[6] The British did indeed furnish considerable assistance; without it, the balance of power in both the Caribbean and, even more, the Philippines, would have been considerably different. Indeed the support provided to Commodore George Dewey's four cruisers on the eve of Manila Bay can be compared with the American support to the British effort in the Falklands nearly one century later. For example, Dewey's squadron was allowed to use Mirs Bay, near Hong Kong, as an advanced base throughout the war. Local British authorities also allowed Dewey to maintain communications to Washington via the trans-Pacific cable in Hong Kong. On the other side of the globe, British authorities prevailed on nominally independent Egypt to deny coaling facilities to Spanish reinforcements on their way to the Far East via the Suez Canal. The Spanish squadron was forced to return to Spain.[7]

The war with Spain gave the United States an overseas empire and great power status. It had clarified the fact also that the United States had become the Western Hemisphere's primary security "broker" – the guns of the US Navy had replaced the British fleet as guardians of the Monroe Doctrine.

As the expansion of the New Navy continued, European, including British statesmen acknowledged that the United States and her navy had become a factor to be reckoned with. Another naval newcomer to be reckoned with by British naval planners was Germany. In 1902, Admiral Sir John Fisher began to prepare the Royal Navy to meet the German threat by, among other things, concentrating its battlefleet in the North Sea. In the Americas, the Pacific squadron virtually disappeared, and the North Atlantic station, based on Halifax, was abolished. Its squadron, now based in Britain, henceforth visited Canada and the Caribbean once a year to "show the flag."

Fisher's decision to denude the American hemisphere of a standing British naval presence was dictated by strategic necessity as well as the recognition that, like it or not, the United States and its navy had become the dominant power in the area. Basic to the British decision was the assumption that, in Fisher's words, the United States was a "kindred state with whom we shall never have a patricidal war."[8] He was correct, of course, but it is important also to stress the *positive* reason for the British decision to acknowledge America's preponderant role in the American seas: it reflected the belief that American and British interests in the area were essentially identical, and that therefore the American wielding of naval power would basically protect British interests as well. Those interests on the eve of World War I were focused on the danger of German penetration of the New World.[9]

In 1901, British Foreign Secretary Lord Lansdowne and his German counterpart, Prince von Bülow, discussed the possibility of an offensive and defensive alliance. The negotiations came to naught for a variety of reasons, one being the British fear of American hostility to a treaty. A memorandum on the negotiations enumerated Germany's global apirations, including those in the American seas. The latter, it was noted, "may safely be left to be dealt with by the United States."[10]

The implicit Anglo-American naval partnership of the nineteenth century became explicit in the next century, when, on 6 April, 1917, both houses of the US Congress voted for war against Germany and its allies. A few weeks afterward six destroyers of the US Atlantic Fleet tied up at the Royal Navy base in Queenstown, Ireland. Four day later, the ships were at sea, teamed up with British destroyers and – a first in American history – under the command of a British officer, Vice Admiral Sir Lewis Bayly, RN. According to some accounts of World War I, it was these destroyers and those that followed that made the convoy system possible. If so, the US Navy can fairly take credit for making the difference in the war's outcome.

The American decision to intervene and tilt the European balance had far-reaching implications that stretched beyond the immediate hostilities: the United States had "come of age" and recognized that its own and the American region's security hinged on global security. The United States henceforth had a stake in the Eurasian balance of power. Hans Morgenthau observed in a book, published in 1947, that the US and British interests in the maintenance of the European balance of power have been "historically identical."[11] The American participation in World War I gave notice that the country had become capable and was prepared to defend this parallel interest with force, if necessary.

Naturalness and Necessity

The "naturalness" of the Anglo-American partnership at sea is embedded in a common heritage and culture, a shared interest in international stability, and, as is remarked upon again later, a *tradition* of cooperation.[12] But what about the "necessary" part of this partnership? More to the point, given the demise of America's Cold War superpower competitor and the country's consequent status as the sole remaining superpower, why should the United States and its navy find the British "sea link" necessary? Cold statistics alone suggest little, if any reason for US Navy dependence on its Royal Navy counterpart. For example, the US Navy's (including Marine Corps) budget authority alone for fiscal year 1997 amounted to nearly $74 billion.[13] This is more than twice the size of Great Britain's entire defense budget in 1997.[14] Looked at in another way, the US Navy's budget in 1997 totalled about one-half of all the 1997 European NATO defense budgets combined.[15] The US-U.K. naval balance reflects this vast budget disparity. The 1997-98 edition of *The Military Balance* reports a US Navy combatant inventory of 18 SSBNs, 75 general purpose submarines, 12 aircraft carriers, 131 cruisers, destroyers, and frigates, and 42 major amphibious vessels. The Royal Navy is credited with three SSBNs, 12 general purpose submarines, three small aircraft carriers, 35 destroyers and frigates, and seven major amphibious ships.[16] So what is it that British naval power can contribute?

"They Seem the Best Prepared for Naval Warfare"

Nation states sign formal alliances, form less formal coalitions, or as has been said of the Anglo-American link, engage in a "common law marriage," for a variety of reasons.[17] But the ultimate purpose is political. After all, if Clausewitz's "discovery" some 160 years ago that war is an extension of politics remains valid, then the instruments of war, i.e. armies, navies, and air forces, must also be political, and the decision by two or more nations to pool those instruments must be politically motivated as well. Two political reasons in particular stand out why a major military power, such as the United States, seeks the active military collaboration of a smaller power, such as Great Britain. First, precisely because in the eyes of the world the United States appears to have the military wherewithal to go-it-alone in most circumstances, it is important that American military action not be seen as the selfish response to "narrow" US interests; that it be seen instead as part of an *international* response to an *international* concern. Secondly and partly related, the threat of military action by a coalition, or to be more precise, a threat by a *credible* coalition, is probably a more effective deterrent to a potential wrongdoer than a unilateral US threat. A multinational military warning is *ipso facto* evidence that the stakes are higher than the US interest alone. A combined Anglo-American "signal" to a would be-aggressor carries particular weight in light of (a) the long history of the transatlantic military partnership and (b) the reputation of British war-fighting efficiency.

What about this reputation, especially among US Navy officers? How do US Navy officers - the people who have to do the actual cooperating on the deckplates - view their service's long "common law marriage" with the Royal Navy? In order to try and get at the answer, a brief, informal survey was circulated among junior US Navy officers (lieutenants, lieutenant commanders) who are pursuing courses of study at the Naval Postgraduate School in Monterey, CA. Student officers were asked to respond in writing to the five written questions below, which they were told were part of a study of multi-national naval cooperation. They questions were these:

1. Suppose you are in a "real" shooting war. Which foreign navy would you prefer fighting on your side?

2. Why?

3. Which capabilities of your preferred naval ally would you want especially on your side? Surface combatants, aviation, submarines, mine warfare forces, others?

4. Have you ever operated with your foreign navy of choice?

5. Where have you spent most of your deployed sea time? Indian Ocean, Western Pacific, Mediterranean?

Altogether 54 responses were received; 39 chose the Royal Navy as their preferred fighting partner. Parenthetically, of those who chose another foreign navy, five preferred another English-speaking service (Australia, Canada, New Zealand). This is a clue as to one of the reasons given for their preference: common language. Other frequently cited reasons included these: (1) professionalism, (2) common style and war-fighting culture, (3) common standard operating procedures and interoperability, (4) quality equipment, (5) the Royal Navy's "tradition of winning," and (6) Britain's dependability/ reliability as an ally and a "history of cooperation."

As to the question of which foreign navy capabilities in particular the respondents would want on their side, no obvious preference was shown. Somewhat surprising perhaps, mine warfare capabilities were rarely cited. Slightly less than one-half of the respondents had had an opportunity to work professionally with Royal Navy units. Since a considerably larger number (72 percent) of the respondents picked the Royal Navy as their ally-of-choice, this suggests that the US Navy officer's preference is based, in part, on British seagoing *reputation*. Finally, the number of officers who had spent most of their seagoing deployments in the Indian Ocean/Western Pacific vs. the Mediterranean was equally divided.[18]

One of the more interesting reasons offered by those who preferred the Royal Navy as their sea-fighting partner was the Anglo-American naval "history of cooperation," or as one respondent put it, "because we are allies." While running the risk of reading perhaps too much between the lines, its suggests that at least some US Navy officers perceive wartime collaboration with their British colleague as the expected, "normal" state of affairs, i.e. "we chose the British because we have always chosen the British." If this is so, Alfred Thayer Mahan would be pleased; his proposal, one century ago, that the United States and Britain team up in an informal "transnational naval consortium" would have become a reality in fact.[19]

Conclusion: Will Technology Put the Partnership at Risk?

In his "Partnership... from the Sea" address Admiral Boorda stressed how the foundation for a successful naval partnership in war must be laid, or as he put it, "nurtured and cared for," in peacetime.[20] The Anglo-American naval partnership has been nourished and strengthened, over the decades, by way of a wide variety of cooperative undertakings - routine navy-to-navy staff talks, combined exercises, officer exchanges, common research and development programs, intelligence sharing, and so forth. All are aimed at ensuring operational interoperability, so that, should the two navies find themselves in harm's way, they will fight as *one*. Operational interoperability involves mutual understanding of how partners operate, how they accomplish different tasks, and the ability to support each other tactically.[21] Effective and efficient interoperability depends on equipment standardization. At a minimum this means that different national systems do not interfere with each other; ideally, partner navies operate common equipments.[22] US and Royal Navy planners today must be on guard that the rapid pace of technological change will not produce system - and thereby operational - asymmetries which could put their long partnership at risk.

These are not idle words. The American military, including its seagoing component, are poised to exploit what has become popularly known as a "Revolution in Military Affairs" (RMA). There is little consensus on what exactly is involved and how this RMA will ultimately re-shape American military capabilities. It is agreed, however, that central to those capabilities will be current and foreseeable improvements in sensor, communication, and computer technologies. A growing number of military professionals and analysts believe - and among America's allies, fear - that, if the RMA is consumated, the result will be a range of American military capabilities beyond the reach of even the most technologically advanced of America's allies. The resulting asymmetries need not spell the end of the Anglo-American naval partnership; it would, however, be a *different* partnership in which respective roles would depend on the contingency at hand. For example, capability asymmetries might not matter greatly if the mission took place in a relatively benign environment, says, an evacuation of nationals; the two partners would effectively act as equals. A more hierarchical relationship would evolve as the environment became more lethal; British naval forces might find themselves in the same side-lined, "also ran" position as Third World forces are today with respect to Anglo-American forces. The Anglo-American partners, especially the Americans will need to decide soon how much interoperability they are willing to sacrifice for the sake of technological innovation.

*   The paraphrase, "Natural and Necessary Allies," is borrowed from Jeremy Black's book, *Natural and Necessary Enemies: Anglo-French Relations in the Eighteenth Century*. Athens, The University of Georgia Press, 1986.

1   ADM J.M. Boorda, US Navy, "Partnership...from the Sea." Address before the International Sea Power Symposium," Newport, 6 November, 1995.

2   *Ibid.*, p. 6.

3   Cited in Geoffrey Warner, "The Anglo-American Special Relationship" in Lawrence S. Kaplan, et. al. Eds., *NATO after Forty Years*. Wilmington, Scholarly Resources, 1990, p. 49.

4   Cited in Forrest Davis, *The Atlantic System: The Story of Anglo-American Control of the Sea* (Cited hereafter as *The Atlantic System*). Westport, Greenwood Press, 1973, p. XII. The book was first published by Reynal & Hitchcock, New York in 1941.

5   Representative Thomas A.E. Weadock, *Congressional Record*, 53:3, p. 2259. Cited in Peter Trubowitz, "Geography and Strategy, The Politics of American Naval Expansion." Paper presented at the SSRC-MacArthur Foundation Workshop, "The Politics of Strategic Adjustment: Ideas, Institutions, and Interests," University of Texas at Austin, Austin, TX, 23–24 April, 1994, p. 16.

6   Cited in *The Atlantic System*, pp. 83–84.

7   Bradford Perkins, *The Great Rapprochement: England and the United States, 1895–1914* (Cited Hereafter as *The Great Rapprochement*). New York, Atheneum, 1968, pp. 45–46. One interesting episode suggestive, if less than factual, of the warming Anglo-American navy–to–navy relationship at the time ocurred at Manila Bay. When Dewey bombarded Manila to soften up the city, two ships of the observing British squadron appeared to place themsdelves deliberately between the Americans and the also observing German squadron. The – unsubstantiated – story has it that in doing so the British saved Dewey from a German stab in the back. *The Great Rapprochement*, p. 47.

8   *Ibid.*, p. 158.

9   *Ibid.*, p. 160.

10   Cited in *The Atlantic System*, p. 127.

11   Hans J. Morgenthau, *In Defense of the National Interest*. New York, Alfred A. Knopf, 1951, p. 115.

12   George Liska's classic study of the dynamics alliance-making (and

breaking) made this observation on the difference between America's alliance relationships with Britain and other nations: "(the) similarities of attitudes of the two English-speaking nations have been more solidly rooted in common philosophic, religious, and common-law traditions as well as their insular stations. They have been nurtured by long and intimate relations between the United States and Britain and by the long predominant role of 'Anglo-Saxon' elites in the making of American foreign policy." *Nations in Alliance: The Limits of Interdependence*, 2d printing. Baltimore, The Johns Hopkins University Press, 1968, pp. 4–5.

13   Navy League of the United States, *Sea Power*, January 1997, p. 89.

14   The 1997–98 issue of *The Military Balance* reports a 1997 British defense budget of $35,904 billion. London, International Institute for Strategic Studies, 1997, p. 34.

15   According to *The Military Balance 1997–98*, the combined 1997 defense budgets for NATO Europe totalled $144,447 billion.

16   *The Military Balance 1997–98*, pp. 20–21, 70–71.

17   For a classic study of why nations align, see Liska, *op. cit.*, especially pp. 26–41.

18   The respondents in this survey were junior US Navy officers. A more in-depth investigation of US Navy officer attitudes toward potential allies would want to compare the views of senior officers. It would also be valuable to conduct a similar survey among Royal Navy and other allied officers.

19   For a recent study of Mahan's advocacy of an Anglo-American naval consortium, see Jon Tetsuro Sumida, *Inventing Grand Strategy and Teaching Command: The Classic Works of Alfred Thayer Mahan Reconsiderted*. Baltimore and London, The Johns Hopkins University Press, 1997, especially, pp. 73–74, 88–89.

20   "Partnership...from the Sea," p. 6.

21   For a good discussion of interoperability issues, see Michael Johnson with Richard Kohout and Peter Swartz, *Guidelines for the World's Maritime Forces in Conducting Multinational Operations: An Analytic Framework*. Alexandria, Center for Naval Analyses, March 1996, and Michael Johnson, Peter Swartz, and Patrick Roth, *Doctrine for Partnership: A Framework for US Multinational Doctrine*. Alexandria, Center for Naval Analyses, March 1996.

22   See, *Doctrine for Partnership: A Framework for US Multinational Naval Doctrine*, p. 131.

The Royal Navy - into the Next Millenium

Eric Grove

The Royal Navy faces both challenges and opportunities with the election of the new Government. The much heralded "Strategic Defence Review" means a reconsideration of defence priorities, which have been moving significantly - if sometimes uncertainly - in a maritime direction since the end of the Cold War. A self conscious change of policy direction thus might not necessarily be in the Navy's interest. Yet the strategic logic that led to this maritime shift cannot be altered by a change at the top. Indeed, the refreshingly open and far reaching nature of the Review gives the proponents of maritime power every opportunity to demonstrate the need for a *more* whole-hearted shift of UK force posture towards an expeditionary capability with maritime forces at its core.

In a world of uncertainties in which the United Kingdom has little idea where her forces will be engaged next , doing what against whom - and with which allies - the inherent deployability of maritime forces, their flexibility and their reach are all at a premium. Although the Government has committed itself to maintaining the level of Defence expenditure for the next two years and to maintaining current orders, the self acknowledged over-stretch of the defence programme means that some setting of priorities is inevitable. Moreover if the Review is to mean anything it must set clear priorities for medium to long term expenditure. In this context concentrating the above mentioned qualities seems the most logical option, ie. investment in the UK's maritime capabilities.

In no other area is the UK so strong in relative terms. Although The Royal Navy has suffered significant cuts in the 1990s its relative power has probably never been greater since the 1950s. With a Russian Navy whose real operational capability is uncertain, the Royal Navy has some claim to second place in the list of the world's most capable navies across the spectrum of naval tasks , albeit at an order of magnitude below the pre-eminent United States Navy. The

RN's combination of carrier, amphibious and nuclear submarine forces is unique among second rank navies.

The future of the last two of these core capabilities is assured. The amphibious transport helicopter (LPH) HMS *Ocean* is due to commission in the Summer of 1998 and the two new amphibious transport docks (LPDs) are due to appear in the Spring of 2002 (HMS *Albion*) and 2003 (HMS *Bulwark*). The late ordering of these ships by the Major administration means that the old steamers *Fearless* and *Intrepid* must soldier on well into their fourth decades. It is unlikely Intrepid will go to sea again, although she is officially at a month's notice for service. Her doubtful condition is presumably one of the expressions of overstretch that the Defence Review is designed to cure.

Three of the five Royal Fleet Auxiliary manned landing ships logistic (LSLs) are modern or modernised and the service life extension programme (SLEP) should be extended to the remaining two vessels if amphibious capability remains a priority. A welcome further addition to the RFA is *Sea Crusader*, the first of two Ro-Ro transports designed to provide lift for the heavy support for the Joint Rapid Deployment Force (JRDF).

Replacement of the nuclear submarine (SSN) force has begun with the ordering of three *A* class boats with an enhanced weapons capacity compared to existing submarines. This will allow *Tomahawk* cruise missiles to be carried with less impact on torpedo load. The first boat is due in 2006 when it will replace an *S* Class unit. In the meantime the combination of *S* and *T* classes provides a unique capability for a medium power to deploy globally and covertly first class multi-purpose submarines for sea denial, power projection and intelligence gathering tasks. SSNs can also provide vital cover for amphibious and carrier forces, as they did in the Falklands War. The much awaited *Tomahawk* enters service aboard HMS *Splendid* in 1998 and the existing SSNs are undergoing a major weapons system modernisation with new sonars of even higher performance than their predecessors.

The key issue for the future is the fate of the carrier force. The *Invincible* class CVSGs will remain in service until the end of the first decade of the Twenty First century. Their power projection capability is being enhanced by carrying RAF GR7 *Harriers* with their better weapons load and night attack capabilities compared to the Navy's own FA2. The latter remains a most capable anti air and anti-surface ship asset, however, with *Blue Vixen* radar and AMRAAM and *Sea Eagle* missiles. The combination of the two airframes carried in a mobile national asset like a CVSG greatly increases the reach and flexibility of Britain's air power.

The utility of the carrier even in situations like the Adriatic has been clearly demonstrated in the last few years and this has greatly assisted in the argument for a carrier replacement. The current front running plan is to build at least two new ships of around 32,000 tons that will have similar capabilities to the currently overcrowded CVSGs. The aircraft carried will be the Short Take Off Vertical Landing (STOVL) variant of the American Joint Strike Fighter (JSF) in which the US Marine Corps and USAF are also interested to replace the AV-8B *Harrier* and A-10 respectively. This could be a formidable general purpose fighter attack aircraft but the RAF seem currently less than interested in acquiring it. It is to be hoped the RAF will see sense on this issue as the concept of properly joint air groups in carriers seems too good to lose. The alternative, a 'navalised' European Fighter Aircraft operating from larger (40,000 ton) carriers would have disadvantages both of cost and operational flexibility. The Navy might be more keen on the idea if it was more certain of the RAF's commitment to the advantages of sea basing.

The new carriers and their aircraft will enter service in the time frame 2010-2015. They will be operating in battle groups with a new generation escort equipped with sophisticated anti-air warfare missile systems. Currently this still seems to mean the UK-French-Italian Project Horizon 6,500 ton 'frigate' due to enter service around 2005 (an auspicious date for an Anglo-French project!). The British ships will be fitted with different fire control radars from their mainland European sisters, a reflection of the more demanding British operational requirements and a greater emphasis of task group operations. One gets the impression that the Horizon project is faltering somewhat and it would not be too surprising if the new carriers found themselves with AAW escorts equipped with the American *Aegis* system. There are a number of options for the Royal Navy acquiring *Aegis*. These range from purchasing existing *Aegis* cruisers from the USA through building *Aegis* destroyers to American design like the Japanese *Kongo* class to putting the *Aegis* system on a modified Type 23 hull along the lines of the next generation of Spanish, Australian and Taiwanese frigates. Certainly RN *Aegis* ships would have to be manned more leanly than current American practice allows but, as the Royal Australian Navy has found out this is quite possible, even in US built ships.

Whatever he solution, *Aegis* would offer real advantages in commonality for operational integration with US battle groups especially with the arrival of the revolutionary Co-operative Engagement Capability (CEC) that, as Norman Friedman has described elsewhere in this volume, allows ships to engage using remotely obtained data. Also *Aegis* is close to becoming an anti-tactical ballistic missile (ATBM) system. It seems a greater pity than ever that the generous American offer of *Aegis* in the 1980s "Naval Defence Initiative" was not taken up.

Whatever their nature, however, it is to be hoped that the full twelve expected AAW ships will be procured to allow one for one replacement of the existing Type 42s. This might prove tricky as the first Type 42 is reportedly due to decommission in 1998 - replaced by an anti-submarine Type 23 in the post *Options for Change* 35 frigate/destroyer total. The Type 23, excellent though she is in her own terms now a proper combat data system is being installed, is probably not the ship the Naval Staff would be procuring if they had known current strategic conditions a decade ago. She is, however a much more efficient user of personnel than earlier surface combat-ants and one can understand the decision to build the last three, bringing the total to 16 units. A couple of Type 22s (those not equipped for the *Merlin* helicopter) may also be retired as the last Type 23s appear but the very important "Outboard" electronic lis-tening capability of the Batch Two ships should ensure the last four at least a long life alongside the four Batch Three Type 22s.

The *Merlin* ship-borne anti-submarine helicopter is one of the Navy's most expensive programmes and, like the Type 23s designed to carry it to prosecute their towed array sonar contacts, it probably would not be in its present form if it had not been conceived in the latter days of the Cold War as a key asset in the campaign against Soviet submarines. The happy decision to give *Merlin* an active as well as passive sonar capability does, however, greatly increase its utility against the expected submarine threat in the new strategic environment and it would provide a key anti-submarine warfare (ASW) asset in any future operations- perhaps a significant niche filler in a world where the USN is tending to neglect ASW in its concentration on strike and air warfare the littoral context.

Equally important as 'niche fillers" are the mine countermeasures (MCM) forces that proved themselves so effective in the Gulf. The original mine countermeasures improvement plans have been drawn down. The extent of the mid-life updates planned for the *Hunt* class sweeper/hunters has been reduced considerably and four are being modified for Northern Ireland patrol duties . But the seven new *Sandown* class minehunters that the Navy managed to extract from a rather reluctant Major Government will mean MCM strength will still be 21 dedicated, high quality assets with the four Northern Ireland ships as an operational reserve. This is probably enough for current and forseeable circumstances.

The mining threat to the *Trident* force has reduced with the end of the Cold War. *Trident* now has a much broader role than intended and, as described elswhere in this volume it provides the UK with a flexible set of nuclear options well suited to deterring a wide range of mass destruction threats. Operational practices seem to be evolving and it is interesting to note that *Vigilant* entered service in 1997 with one augmented crew rather than the traditional two crews. It is hard to justify traditional alert patterns in the new strategic situation.

The Royal Navy thus provides a spectrum of capabilities across the range from the highest levels of conflict to the lowest. It is capable of projecting power in either a national or, more likely, a coalition context. The 1997 *Ocean Wave* deployment demonstrated clearly the continuing and in some ways expanding reach of the fleet. It is hard to think of a more effective investment of national resources and it seems likely that the Strategic Defence Review will recognise the unique and fundamental contribution Britain's maritime forces make to her continuing role as a leading contributor to the maintenance of international peace and security on a global scale.

INDEX

5, 136-7, 139
Truce Supervision
Organisation (UNTSO)   135
United States   3, 6, 8, 10-12,
  14-5, 29, 37, 41-3, 47-50, 53,
  64, 71-3, 82, 93, 103, 105,
  112-3, 118, 124, 135-6, 141,
  148, 153, 157, 160-6
  Air Force   113, 172
  Army   50
  Civil War   147, 160
United States Marine Corps   15,
  33, 77, 101, 105, 163, 172
United States Navy   28, 32-3,
  43, 46, 49-50, 62, 65, 71-2,
  77-8, 82, 89, 113, 135, 152,
  158-9, 161-6, 170, 173-4
  Forward from the Sea   7
  Maritime Strategy   12, 35
  Naval Postgraduate School
  164
  Naval War College   27
Unmanned Aerial Vehicle (UAV)
  93-4
Unmanned Underwater Vehicle
  (UUV)   92-4
Ushuaia   135
USSR   73, 77, 112
  (see also: Russia; Soviet
  Union)

Vanguard, SSBN class   117
  (see: SLBM; SSBN; Trident)
Venice   34
Vietnam   5
  War   49
Vigilant, HMS   174
  (see: SLBM; SSBN; Trident;
  Vanguard)
Vulcan, bomber   112

Walcheren Island, Battle of   105
Warrior, HMS   148
Warsaw Pact   115
Washington   161
WE177, warhead   114, 118
Weapons of Mass Destruction

(WMD)   8
Western European Union (WEU)
  136-7
West Indies   40
Westkapelle, Battle of   105
West New Guinea   135
Wilhelm, Kaiser II   149
Wilhelmshaven   146
World Bank   3
World War One   38-9, 70-1,
  150, 162-3
World War Two   29-30, 33, 37-
  9, 49, 59, 70, 76, 79, 90, 135,
  159

Yugoslavia   17, 81-2, 103, 136

Zaire   102

DIMENSIONS OF SEA POWER
Strategic Choice in the Modern World